What's Your Red, White & Blue IQ?

What's Your
Red, White & Blue
IQ?

Stephen J. Spignesi

CITADEL PRESS
Kensington Publishing Corp.
www.kensingtonbooks.com

CITADEL PRESS BOOKS are published by

Kensington Publishing Corp.
850 Third Avenue
New York, NY 10022

All Kensington titles, imprints, and distributed lines are available at special quantity discounts for bulk purchases for sales promotions, premiums, fund-raising, educational, or institutional use. Special book excerpts or customized printings can also be created to fit specific needs. For details, write or phone the office of the Kensington special sales manager: Kensington Publishing Corp., 850 Third Avenue, New York, NY 10022, attn: Special Sales Department; phone 1-800-221-2647.

All art courtesy ClipArt.com.

First printing: June 2004

10 9 8 7 6 5

Printed in the United States of America

Library of Congress Control Number: 2004100539

ISBN 0-8065-2625-4

For Ann LaFarge

Contents

I

The American Presidents

II
The American Way

III
The American Military

IV
America at War

☆ Contents ☆

IX

American Holidays

X

Great American Documents

XI

The American Flag

XII

An All-American Potpourri

Introduction:
Three Cheers for the Red, White & Blue!

What's Your Red, White & Blue IQ? is intended to entertain and teach.

There are many quizzes and questions here that are relatively simple and that even a child might answer.

There are quizzes that require very little knowledge of American history whatsoever.

And then there are questions and quizzes that only the most knowledgeable of U.S. history buffs will be able to answer—without turning to books or other resources to discern the answer.

But it is not cheating to go look up a fact in order to answer a question, or questions.

In fact, that is what we encourage you to do.

The study and understanding of American history should be a lifelong pursuit for all Americans.

We live in a wondrous country, a nation founded on a principle that is both simple and profound at the same time: liberty.

How did we come to be?

How did America finally get it right?

What's Your Red, White & Blue IQ? covers everything from the Presidents and America at war to American popular culture and our space program, and everything else in between.

We hope you may come upon an answer of your own to those two important questions as you work your way through these 101 quizzes.

Acknowledgments

John White and Bill Savo must be singled out for their immeasurable assistance with this book.

Ann LaFarge and Bruce Bender also deserve heartfelt thanks for their advice and guidance, as well as Gary Goldstein who stalwartly came aboard at the last minute and performed nobly.

Also, thanks to the University of New Haven, the Library of Congress, the Smithsonian Institution, Mike Lewis, Colin Andrews, Jim Cole, Charlie Fried, Janet Daniw, Michaela Hamilton and everyone at Kensington Books, ClipArt.com, Publishers Marketplace, ABE.com, Emily Resnik-Conn, Mary Toler, Alyse and Rob Geremia, and Laura Lattrell.

Very special thanks to Steve Rapuano.

And as always, Pam, Lee, and Carter.

John Adams's Letter to Abigail Adams, July 3, 1776

Note: *On July 2, 1776, the delegates of twelve colonies voted unanimously to adopt a resolution proposed by Richard Henry Lee of Virginia, which stated: "That these United Colonies are and of right ought to be free and independent states."*

But the day is past. The Second Day of July 1776, will be the most memorable Epocha, in the History of America. I am apt to believe that it will be celebrated, by succeeding Generations, as the great anniversary Festival. It ought to be commemorated, as the Day of Deliverance by solemn Acts of Devotion to God Almighty. It ought to be solemnized with Pomp and Parade, with Shews, Games, Sports, Guns, Bell, Bonfires, and Illuminations from one End of this Continent to the other from This Time forward forever more.

You will think me transported with Enthusiasm but I am not. I am well aware of the Toil and Blood and Treasure, that it will cost Us to maintain this Declaration, and support and defend these States. Yet through all the Gloom I can see the Rays of ravishing light and Glory. I can see that the End is more than worth all the Means. And that Posterity will triumph in that Days Transaction, even altho We should rue it, which I trust in God We shall not.

An Excerpt from George Washington's Last Will and Testament, July 1799

To each of my Nephews, William Augustine Washington, George Lewis, George Steptoe Washington, Bushroe Washington and Samuheir Countrel Washington, I give one of the Swords or Cutteaux of which I may die possessed; and they are to chuse in the order they are named. These Swords are accompanied with an injunction not to unsheath them for the purpose of shedding blood, except it be for self-defense, or in defence of their Country and its rights; and in the latter case, to keep them unsheathed, and prefer falling with them in their hands, to the relinquishment thereof.

What's Your
Red, White & Blue
IQ?

QUIZ 1

Coming to America:
The Immigration Experience

☆ ☆ ☆ ☆ ☆

A great many people from other countries want to come to America. And who can blame them? Over the past century, millions of foreign-born immigrants willingly surrendered their birthplace citizenship to become an American. Answer these questions about the American immigration experience.

1. TRUE OR FALSE: U.S. immigration policy in 1941 forbade aliens from becoming physicians, attorneys, CPAs, pharmacists, dentists, optometrists, teachers, mine inspectors, engineers, bank directors, architects, barbers, master plumbers, and registered nurses.

2. Which of the following comprised the foreign-born population of the United States in the year 2000?
   a. 10.5 million people—3.75 percent of the total U.S. population
   b. 31.1 million people—11.1 percent of the total U.S. population
   c. 56.5 million people—20 percent of the total U.S. population
   d. 73.8 million people—26.3 percent of the total U.S. population

3. Name the country that was the source of the majority of America's immigrants and their descendants.

4. Where is Ellis Island?

5. TRUE OR FALSE: Ellis Island was the chief immigration station for the United States from 1892 to 1943.

6. In the decade from 1991 through 2000, what was the ethnic origin of over half of the foreign-born in America?

   a. Eastern European   c. Canadian

   b. Middle Eastern   d. Latin American

7. What color is a Green Card?

8. Fill in the blank: The Immigration Act of 1921 limited the number of immigrants from any one country in any given year to no more than _____ percent of the number of people who had been born in that country living in the United States in the year 1910.

9. What caused the large influx of immigrants from Ireland beginning in the year 1845?

   a. Free steerage to America

   b. A smallpox epidemic in Ireland

   c. The Irish Potato Famine

   d. Harsh British deportation policies

10. On July 13, 1869, bloody riots broke out in San Francisco against a particular group of immigrants. The violence was caused by resentment against these immigrant laborers who would work for very low wages and take jobs away from native Americans. What nationality were these immigrants?

    a. Mexican   c. Greek

    b. Italian   d. Chinese

I

The American Presidents

QUIZ 2

Which President . . . ?

☆ ☆ ☆ ☆ ☆

1. Which President was the tallest?
   a. Abraham Lincoln
   b. Lyndon B. Johnson
   c. Thomas Jefferson
   d. Bill Clinton
   e. Franklin Delano Roosevelt

Honest Abe Lincoln

2. Which President was *not* a Mason?
   a. James Garfield
   b. Gerald Ford
   c. James Buchanan
   d. George Washington
   e. John F. Kennedy

3. Which President did *not* die in office?
   a. William Henry Harrison
   b. Zachary Taylor
   c. Grover Cleveland
   d. James Garfield
   e. John F. Kennedy

4. Which President was *not* born a British subject?
   a. George Washington
   b. Thomas Jefferson
   c. James Monroe
   d. Martin Van Buren
   e. William Henry Harrison

5. Which President was *not* of the Baptist religious affiliation?
   a. John F. Kennedy
   b. Warren Harding
   c. Harry Truman
   d. Bill Clinton
   e. Jimmy Carter

6. Which President once described himself as "the man who accompanied [his wife] to Paris"?
   a. John Quincy Adams
   b. John Adams
   c. Bill Clinton
   d. John F. Kennedy
   e. James Buchanan

7. Which President once got stuck in a White House bathtub?
   a. Zachary Taylor
   b. William Howard Taft
   c. John Adams
   d. Thomas Jefferson
   e. William Henry Harrison

8. Which President introduced the donkey to America?
   a. Millard Fillmore
   b. Theodore Roosevelt
   c. Ulysses S. Grant
   d. John Tyler
   e. George Washington

9. Which President was a bigamist?
   a. Woodrow Wilson
   b. Chester A. Arthur
   c. Ulysses S. Grant
   d. John Quincy Adams
   e. Andrew Jackson

Theodore "Teddy" Roosevelt

10. Which President fathered fifteen children with two wives?
    a. John Tyler
    b. James Polk
    c. Zachary Taylor
    d. Millard Fillmore
    e. Franklin Pierce

11. Which two Presidents were slaves when they were young boys?

    a. John Adams
    b. Abraham Lincoln
    c. Andrew Johnson
    d. Millard Fillmore
    e. George Washington

12. Which President was the only Chief Executive to remain a bachelor his entire life?

    a. William Howard Taft
    b. James Buchanan
    c. James Garfield
    d. James Polk
    e. Dwight D. Eisenhower

13. Which President was the only President not to have a single day of formal schooling?

    a. Abraham Lincoln
    b. Andrew Johnson
    c. Herbert Hoover
    d. William McKinley
    e. John Quincy Adams

14. Which President could simultaneously write Greek with one hand and Latin with the other?

    a. George Washington
    b. John Adams
    c. Thomas Jefferson
    d. James Garfield
    e. Abraham Lincoln

15. Which President insisted that his morning egg be boiled for thirty minutes?

    a. Ronald Reagan
    b. John F. Kennedy
    c. Richard Nixon
    d. Woodrow Wilson
    e. Bill Clinton

16. Which President was inducted into the Ku Klux Klan at a White House ceremony?

    a. James Monroe
    b. James Polk
    c. Andrew Jackson
    d. Warren G. Harding
    e. Andrew Johnson

17. Which President once lost a complete set of White House china in a poker game?
    a. Warren G. Harding
    b. Jimmy Carter
    c. Gerald Ford
    d. Franklin Pierce
    e. Andrew Johnson

18. Which President loved to have his head rubbed with Vaseline while he ate breakfast in bed?
    a. Ronald Reagan
    b. Bill Clinton
    c. Jimmy Carter
    d. Grover Cleveland
    e. Calvin Coolidge

19. Which President was confirmed by genealogists to have been related to eleven Presidents: George Washington, the two Adams, James Madison, Martin Van Buren, the two Harrisons, John Taylor, Ulysses S. Grant, Theodore Roosevelt, and William Howard Taft?
    a. John F. Kennedy
    b. Harry Truman
    c. Dwight D. Eisenhower
    d. Franklin Delano Roosevelt
    e. Bill Clinton

20. Which President once insulted all of Mexico by admitting that he had gotten diarrhea during a stay in Mexico City?
    a. Gerald Ford
    b. Jimmy Carter
    c. Bill Clinton
    d. George W. Bush
    e. George Bush

QUIZ 3

Presidential Milestones

☆ ☆ ☆ ☆ ☆

George Washington—the first President

Match the President in the left column with one of his administration's milestones from the right column.

1. George Washington

2. John Adams

3. Thomas Jefferson

4. James Madison

5. James Monroe

6. John Quincy Adams

7. Andrew Jackson

8. Martin Van Buren

a. The Iran-Contra Scandal

b. Pearl Harbor

c. The Persian Gulf War

d. The Emancipation Proclamation

e. The Panama Canal

f. The Stock Market Crash and the Great Depression

g. The Air Commerce Act

9. William Henry Harrison	h. The Compromise of 1850
10. John Tyler	i. The Tariff of Abominations
11. James Polk	j. The My Lai Massacre
12. Zachary Taylor	k. Whip Inflation Now
13. Millard Fillmore	l. The Federal Trade Commission (FTC)
14. Franklin Pierce	
15. James Buchanan	m. Operation Iraqi Freedom
16. Abraham Lincoln	n. The Annexation of Texas
17. Andrew Johnson	o. The Panic of 1857
18. Ulysses S. Grant	p. The Camp David Accord
19. Rutherford B. Hayes	q. Charles Guiteau
20. James Garfield	r. The Spanish-American War
21. Chester A. Arthur	s. Wounded Knee
22. Grover Cleveland	t. The Pendelton Act of 1883
23. Benjamin Harrison	u. The Interstate Commerce Act of 1887
24. Grover Cleveland	
25. William McKinley	v. The Constitutional Convention
26. Theodore Roosevelt	w. Impeachment
27. William Howard Taft	x. The one-month Presidency
28. Woodrow Wilson	y. The Panic of 1837
29. Warren G. Harding	z. The Panic of 1873
30. Calvin Coolidge	aa. Hiroshima
31. Herbert Hoover	bb. The War of 1812
32. Franklin D. Roosevelt	cc. Forty-eight contiguous states for the first time
33. Harry S. Truman	

34. Dwight D. Eisenhower

35. John F. Kennedy

36. Lyndon B. Johnson

37. Richard Nixon

38. Gerald Ford

39. Jimmy Carter

40. Ronald Reagan

41. George Bush

42. Bill Clinton

43. George W. Bush

dd. NASA

ee. The Panic of 1893

ff. The Compromise of 1877

gg. The Cuban Missile Crisis

hh. The Teapot Dome Scandal

ii. Monica Lewinsky

jj. The Gadsden Purchase of 1853

kk. The Clayton-Bulwer Treaty of 1850

ll. The Indian Removal Act

mm. The XYZ Affair

nn. The Declaration of Independence

oo. The Missouri Compromise

pp. Manifest Destiny

qq. Resignation

QUIZ 4

The Presidents and Their Wars

☆ ☆ ☆ ☆ ☆

Match the war from the left column with the President or Presidents under whose administration the war was waged from the right column.

1. Revolutionary War (1775–1783)

2. Spanish-American War (1898–1899)

3. World War I (1917–1918)

4. Civil War (1861–1865)

5. War Against Terrorism (2001–)

6. Persian Gulf War (1990–1991)

7. War of 1812

8. Vietnam War (1964–1973)

9. Indian Wars (1865–1898)

10. Korean War (1950–1953)

11. World War II (1941–1945)

12. Mexican War (1846–1848)

a. William McKinley

b. Abraham Lincoln

c. James Madison

d. George H.W. Bush

e. Lyndon Johnson, Richard Nixon

f. James Polk

g. Woodrow Wilson

h. Franklin Delano Roosevelt, Harry Truman

i. Harry Truman, Dwight D. Eisenhower

j. George Washington[1]

k. William McKinley, Theodore Roosevelt

l. George W. Bush

13. Philippine War (1898–1902)   m. Andrew Johnson, Ulysses S. Grant, Rutherford B. Hayes, James Garfield, Chester A. Arthur, Grover Cleveland, Benjamin Harrison, William McKinley

QUIZ 5

On the Road Again

☆ ☆ ☆ ☆ ☆

This quiz asks you to identify the President from information provided about his travels. A hint: Often, the time period of the trips is provided in the question and the Presidential Reference Appendix may assist you in narrowing down the specific administration and, therefore, the President in question.

1. This President visited Cuba in January 1928 to address the Sixth International Conference of American States. This was his only trip abroad as President of the United States.

2. This President visited the Korean combat zone in December 1952 as President-elect, and during his administration, he met with China's President Chiang Kai-Shek, Mexico's President Lopes Mateos, Soviet Premier Kruschev, and France's President De Gaulle. He also had an audience with Pope John XXIII and once addressed a joint session of Canada's Parliament.

3. This President loved vacationing on Campobello Island in Canada, and also made several fishing trips to the Bahamas during his term in office.

4. This President attended the funeral of Japan's Emperor Hirohito, had an audience with Pope John Paul II, and visited international relief workers and U.S. military personnel in Somalia.

5. This President visited with France's Jacques Chirac two months before an assassination attempt was made against the French President during a Bastille Day parade.

6. This President met with Spain's Generalissimo Franco and received the keys to the city of Madrid from its mayor. He also once met with Romania's brutal dictator President Ceausescu and the Philippines' equally vile Ferdinand Marcos.

7. This President met with Winston Churchill and Joseph Stalin at Potsdam, Germany.

8. This President was the first U.S. President to visit the President of a sub-Saharan African nation. He also met with Egyptian President Sadat before Sadat was assassinated, and signed the SALT I treaty with Soviet General Secretary Brezhnev.

9. This President described himself as the man who accompanied his wife to Paris.

10. This President visited U.S. military personnel in Vietnam during the Vietnam War.

11. This President attended Charles De Gaulle's funeral; signed the SALT II treaty in Moscow, and had an audience with Pope Paul VI.

12. This President visited his ancestral home in Ireland, attended commemorative ceremonies of the fortieth anniversary of the Allied landing in Normandy, and had an audience with Pope John Paul II.

13. This President made the first trip abroad by a U.S. President when he visited Panama to inspect the construction of the Panama Canal.

14. This Rhodes Scholar President attended the signing of the Israel-Jordan peace agreement in Jordan and addressed the Jordanian Parliament. He also attended the funeral of Israeli Prime Minister Yitzhak Rabin and visited the Great Barrier Reef in Australia.

15. This President had an audience with Pope Benedict XV, the only U.S. President to ever meet with the early twentieth-century Pontiff.

Presidential Pens

☆ ☆ ☆ ☆ ☆

Match the President from the left column with the book he wrote from the right column.

1. John Adams

2. Thomas Jefferson

3. James Monroe

4. John Quincy Adams

5. Grover Cleveland

6. Benjamin Harrison

7. William McKinley

8. Theodore Roosevelt

9. William Howard Taft

10. Woodrow Wilson

11. Herbert C. Hoover

12. Franklin D. Roosevelt

13. Harry S. Truman

14. Dwight D. Eisenhower

15. John F. Kennedy

16. Lyndon B. Johnson

a. *Dermot MacMorrogh or, The Conquest of Ireland: An Historical Tale of the Twelfth Century* (poetry, 1832)

b. *Rough Riders* (1899)

c. *A History of the American People* (five volumes, 1902)

d. *Fishing and Shooting Sketches* (1904)

e. *Mr. Citizen* (1960)

f. *Profiles in Courage* (1956)

g. *Notes on the State of Virginia* (1785)

h. *Six Crises* (1962)

i. *Portrait of an Assassin* (1976)

j. *At Ease: Stories I Tell to Friends* (1967)

17. Richard M. Nixon

18. Gerald R. Ford

19. Jimmy Carter, Jr.

20. Ronald W. Reagan

21. George H. W. Bush

22. William J. Clinton

k. *Man of Integrity* (1988)

l. *Principles of Mining* (1909)

m. *Putting People First* (1992)

n. *This Country of Ours* (1897)

o. *Four Aspects of Civic Duty* (1906)

p. *An American Life: The Autobiography* (1990)

q. *The Tariff in the Days of Henry Clay and Since* (1896)

r. *Always a Reckoning and Other Poems* (1995)

s. *A Defense of the Constitutions of Government of the United States of America* (three volumes, 1787–1788)

t. *The Vantage Point: Perspectives of the Presidency, 1963–1969* (1971)

u. *The Happy Warrior, Alfred E. Smith* (1928)

v. *A View of the Conduct of the Executive in the Foreign Affairs of the United States* (1797)

QUIZ 7

Last Words

☆ ☆ ☆ ☆ ☆

Identify the President for each of the "last words."

1. "Doctor, I am going. Perhaps it is best." _____

2. "Good-bye. Good-bye to all. It is God's will. His will, not ours, be done." _____

3. "I am a broken piece of machinery. When the machinery is broken . . . I am ready." _____

4. "I am about to die. I expect the summons very soon. I have tried to discharge my duties faithfully. I regret nothing, but I am sorry that I am about to leave my friends." _____

5. "I am just going. Have me decently buried and do not let my body be put into a vault in less than two days after I am dead. Do you understand me? 'Tis well." _____

6. "I have a terrific headache." _____

7. "I have tried so hard to do right." _____

8. "I know that I am going where Lucy is." _____

9. "I want to go; God take me." _____

10. "I wish you to understand the true principles of the Government. I wish them carried out. I ask nothing more." _____

11. "Is it the Fourth?" _____

12. "Nothing more than a change of *mind*, my dear."

_____

17

13. "Oh, do not cry. Be good children, and we shall all meet in Heaven." _____

14. "Please put out the light." _____

15. "Swaim, can't you stop this? Oh, Swaim!" _____

16. "That is very obvious." _____

17. "That's good. Go on; read some more." _____

18. "This is the end of earth," followed by either, "but I am composed" or, "I am content." _____

19. "Thomas Jefferson still survives." _____

20. "Water." _____

QUIZ 8

Presidential Nicknames

☆ ☆ ☆ ☆ ☆

U.S. Presidents seem to be the Rodney Dangerfields of American politics: sometimes, they get no respect. Match the President from the left column with the oftentimes insulting and merciless nickname from the right column.

1.	George Washington	a.	Big Beefhead
2.	John Adams	b.	His Rotundity
3.	Thomas Jefferson	c.	The Fainting General
4.	James Madison	d.	Old Eight to Seven
5.	James Monroe	e.	The Illinois Baboon
6.	John Quincy Adams	f.	The Buffalo Hangman
7.	Andrew Jackson	g.	The Puritan
8.	Martin Van Buren	h.	Old Rough and Ready
9.	William Henry Harrison	i.	The American Louis Philippe
10.	John Tyler	j.	Four Eyes
11.	James K. Polk	k.	The Happy Warrior
12.	Zachary Taylor	l.	The Dumb Prophet
13.	Millard Fillmore	m.	The Sage of the Hermitage
14.	Franklin Pierce	n.	Big Bill
15.	James Buchanan	o.	The Napoleon of Protection
16.	Abraham Lincoln	p.	Deficit

17. Andrew Johnson
18. Ulysses S. Grant
19. Rutherford B. Hayes
20. James A. Garfield
21. Chester A. Arthur
22. Grover Cleveland
23. Benjamin Harrison
24. William McKinley
25. Theodore Roosevelt
26. William Howard Taft
27. Woodrow Wilson
28. Warren G. Harding
29. Calvin Coolidge
30. Herbert C. Hoover
31. Franklin D. Roosevelt
32. Harry S. Truman
33. Dwight D. Eisenhower
34. John F. Kennedy
35. Lyndon B. Johnson
36. Richard M. Nixon
37. Gerald Ford
38. Jimmy Carter
39. Ronald Reagan
40. George Bush
41. William Jefferson Clinton
42. George W. Bush

q. Machievellian Belshazzar
r. The Featherduster of Duchess County
s. The Sharp Knife
t. Long Tom
u. The American Fabius
v. Jack
w. Gloomy Gus
x. The Haberdasher
y. The Great Communicator
z. His Accidency
aa. Houdini in the White House
bb. Poppy
cc. The Old Lion
dd. The Canal Boy
ee. Mr. Big
ff. The Napoleon of the Stump
gg. Big Daddy
hh. The Teflon President
ii. The Shadow of Blooming Grove
jj. Silent Cal
kk. The Daddy of the Baby
ll. Dubya
mm. Bubba

nn. Jimmy

oo. Jerry

pp. The Bachelor President

qq. The Mistletoe Politician

rr. The Lost Cocked Hat

ss. The Phrasemaker

tt. The Iron Butt

uu. Ike

vv. The Butcher from Galena

ww. Unconditional Surrender

xx. The Sphinx

yy. A Traitor to His Class

zz. The Chief

aaa. Petticoat Pet

bbb. The Schoolmaster

ccc. Little Jamie

ddd. Kid Gloves

eee. The Trust-Buster

fff. Old Granny

ggg. The Stocking-Foot Orator

hhh. Uncle Jumbo

iii. The Old Fox

jjj. The Dude

kkk. Old Man Eloquent

lll. Useless

QUIZ 9

Presidential Burial Places

☆ ☆ ☆ ☆ ☆

Two Presidents are buried in Arlington National Cemetery. Seven Presidents are buried in New York; five are buried in Ohio; four are buried in Virginia; three are buried in Tennessee. One President is interred in the Washington National Cathedral.

Match the President from the left column with the place where he is buried from the right column. **Note:** From No. 22, "Grover Cleveland" on, the numbers do not reflect the chronological order of the President's administration. Since Cleveland was the twenty-second *and* the twenty-fourth President, but could only be buried once, he is assigned a single spot and the remaining (deceased) Presidents are numbered chronologically from that point on.

1. George Washington
2. John Adams
3. Thomas Jefferson
4. James Madison
5. James Monroe
6. John Quincy Adams
7. Andrew Jackson
8. Martin Van Buren
9. William Henry Harrison
10. John Tyler
11. James K. Polk

a. Abilene, Kansas
b. Albany, New York
c. Arlington National Cemetery
d. Buffalo, New York
e. Canton, Ohio
f. Charlottesville, Virginia
g. Cleveland, Ohio
h. Concord, New Hampshire
i. Fremont, Ohio
j. Greeneville, Tennessee
k. Hyde Park, New York

22

12. Zachary Taylor		l.	Independence, Missouri
13. Millard Fillmore		m.	Indianapolis, Indiana
14. Franklin Pierce		n.	Johnson City, Texas
15. James Buchanan		o.	Kinderhook, New York
16. Abraham Lincoln		p.	Lancaster, Pennsylvania
17. Andrew Johnson		q.	Louisville, Kentucky
18. Ulysses S. Grant		r.	Marion, Ohio
19. Rutherford B. Hayes		s.	Montpelier Station, Vermont
20. James A. Garfield			
21. Chester A. Arthur		t.	Mt. Vernon, Virginia
22. Grover Cleveland		u.	Nashville, Tennessee
23. Benjamin Harrison		v.	New York, New York
24. William McKinley		w.	North Bend, Ohio
25. Theodore Roosevelt		x.	Oyster Bay, New York
26. William Howard Taft		y.	Plymouth, Vermont
27. Woodrow Wilson		z.	Princeton, New Jersey
28. Warren G. Harding		aa.	Quincy, Massachusetts
29. Calvin Coolidge		bb.	Richmond, Virginia
30. Herbert C. Hoover		cc.	Springfield, Illinois
31. Franklin D. Roosevelt		dd.	Washington National Cathedral
32. Harry S. Truman		ee.	West Branch, Iowa
33. Dwight D. Eisenhower		ff.	Yorba Linda, California
34. John F. Kennedy			
35. Lyndon B. Johnson			
36. Richard M. Nixon			

II

The American Way

QUIZ 10

Our American Government: Part 1

☆ ☆ ☆ ☆ ☆

In 2000, our American government published a booklet titled *Our American Government.*

This booklet, free to all for the asking, was an official publication of the 106th Congress, 2nd session. It was known as House Document 106-216, and it was printed by authority of House Resolution 221.

This booklet is a gold mine of information about . . . well, about our American government. It contains 178 informative questions and answers about American government, plus a lengthy glossary, an equally complete bibliography, the complete texts of the Declaration of Independence, and the Constitution (with all the Amendments), an Index, and a slew of other valuable resources.

Since one of the purposes of *What's Your Red, White & Blue IQ?* is to instruct as well as entertain, we have culled twenty-one key questions and answers from *Our American Government* for these three quizzes. (The Legislative Glossary matching quiz is also drawn from *Our American Government.*)

You should try to answer these questions in your own words, to the best of your knowledge. As you will see when you get to the Answers section, the answers to these twenty-one questions (which are reproduced verbatim from the government booklet) are quite detailed and, in some cases, somewhat lengthy. You are not, of course, expected to be able to parrot the official answers, but you should try to respond with as much information as you can to answer the questions. We guarantee that reading the answers will be an enlightening learning experience.

If these twenty-one questions intrigue (and we hope they do), *Our American Government* can be obtained from the Government Printing Office.

No home, office, or school should be without one.

Our American Government is available online at:

frwebgate.access.gpo.gov/cgi-bin/getdoc.cgi?dbname=106_cong_documents&docid=f:hd216.106

It is available for a $3 charge from the Government Printing Office bookstore at bookstore.gpo.gov/

1. What form of government do we have in the United States?

2. What contributions has our country made to the institution of government?

3. What were the basic principles on which the Constitution was framed?

4. How may the Constitution be amended?

5. What is the "lame duck" amendment?

QUIZ 11

Our American Government: Part 2

1. What is meant by the "separation of powers" and "checks and balances" in the Federal Government?

2. What are the duties of the officers and senior officials of the House?

3. Who presides over the Senate?

4. What are party leaders?

5. What is the congressional budget process?

Our American Government: Part 3

1. What is the difference between an authorization and an appropriation?

2. What organizations are included in the legislative branch?

3. What is the procedure to commit the country's military force to war?

4. How is the President addressed?

5. What is the wording of the oath taken by the President? Who administers it?

6. What would happen if the President-elect were to die before taking office?

7. What is the main principle of the system of justice in the United States?

8. Why is so much importance placed on a Supreme Court decision?

9. How much may candidates spend on their campaign for federal office?

10. How is a request for records made under the Freedom of Information Act?

BONUS. What are the stages of a bill in Congress? (**Note:** This is a tough one, since there are fourteen stages of a bill in Congress. Try to come up with as many as you can. If you get a high number, either you are a politician, a political science graduate student, or you watch an enormous amount of *The West Wing*.)

QUIZ 13

A Legislative Glossary Quiz

☆ ☆ ☆ ☆ ☆

Match the legislative term from the left column with its correct definition from the right column. (All definitions taken verbatim or paraphrased from the U.S. Government publication, *Our American Government*.)

1. Act

2. Advice and Consent

3. Bipartisanship

4. Caucus

5. Cloture

6. Confirmation

7. Contempt of Congress

8. Continuing Resolution

9. Filibuster

10. Germaneness

11. Hearing

12. Joint Meeting

13. Joint Session

a. A group organized to promote its members' views on selected issues, usually through raising money that is contributed to the campaign funds of candidates who support the group's position.

b. A House rule that amendments to a bill must relate to the subject matter under consideration.

c. A joint appropriations measure providing emergency funding for agencies whose regular appropriations bill has not been passed.

d. A meeting of both Houses of Congress, customarily held in the House Chamber, held for necessary administrative and official purposes, e.g., the purpose of counting electoral votes, attending inaugurations, and to hear Presidential State of the Union messages.

14. Markup

15. Memorial

16. Petition

17. Political Action
    Committee (PAC)

18. Quorum

19. Ratification

20. Rider

21. Session

22. *Sine Die*

23. Tabling Motion

24. Unanimous
    Consent

25. Veto

e. A meeting of both Houses of
Congress, in which each Chamber
recesses to meet for an occasion or
ceremony, usually in the House
Chamber.

f. A meeting of Democratic Party
members in the House, which elects
party leaders and makes decisions
on legislative business.

g. A meeting or session of a committee
of Congress—usually open to the
public—to obtain information and
opinions on proposed legislation, to
conduct an investigation, or oversee
a program.

h. A motion to stop action on a
pending proposal and to lay it aside
indefinitely.

i. A parliamentary device used in the
Senate by which debate on a
particular measure can be limited.

j. A petition to Congress from State
legislatures, usually requesting some
sort of legislation, or expressing the
sense of the State legislature on a
particular question.

k. A practice in the House and Senate
to set aside a rule of procedure, so
as to expedite proceedings.

l. A process of Senate approval of
executive and judicial appointments,
and for treaties negotiated by the
executive branch and signed by the
President.

m. A request or plea sent to one or both Houses from an organization or private citizens' group asking support of particular legislation or favorable consideration of a matter.

n. Action by the Senate, approving Presidential nominees for the executive branch, regulatory commissions, and certain other positions.

o. An unrelated amendment attached to a pending bill in order to improve its chances for passage.

p. Cooperation between members of both political parties in either or both Houses, or between the President and Members of Congress representing the other party in addressing a particular issue or proposal.

q. Debate typically characterized by individual Senators or groups of Senators speaking at extended length against a pending measure, often with the objective of frustrating action on the pending legislative proposals.

r. Either the act of approval of a proposed constitutional amendment by the legislatures of the States, or the Senate process of advice and consent to treaties negotiated by the President.

s. Legislation which has passed both
Houses of Congress, approved by
the president, or passed over his
veto, thus becoming law.

t. The consitutional procedure by
which the President refuses to
approve a bill or joint resolution and
thus prevents its enactment into law.

u. The final adjournment used to
conclude a session of Congress.

v. The number of Members in each
House necessary to conduct
business.

w. The period during which Congress
assembles and carries on its regular
business.

x. The process in which congressional
committees and subcommittees
amend and rewrite proposed
legislation in order to prepare it for
consideration on the floor.

y. Willful obstruction of the legislative
process.

QUIZ 14

How Well Do You Know Washington, D.C.?

☆ ☆ ☆ ☆ ☆

1. TRUE OR FALSE: The Arlington Memorial Bridge crosses the Potomac River and connects the site of the Lincoln Memorial with Arlington National Cemetery.

2. Which of the following sites are in Arlington National Cemetery?
   a. The Iwo Jima Memorial
   b. The Taft Grave
   c. The Kennedy Gravesites
   d. The Tomb of the Unknowns
   e. The Confederate Memorial
   f. All of the above

3. TRUE OR FALSE: The Capitol Reflecting Pool is in front of the Lincoln Memorial.

4. What is the name of the fresco adorning the dome canopy of the U.S. Capitol Rotunda?
   a. *The Death of Washington*
   b. *The Apotheosis of Washington*
   c. *George Washington*
   d. *Democracy*

5. Who painted the fresco adorning the dome canopy of the U.S. Capitol Rotunda while lying on his back?
   a. Constantino Brumidi
   b. Antonio Garibaldi
   c. Francesco Mandato
   d. Sebastiano Rapuano

6. TRUE OR FALSE: Anyone can visit the Supreme Court and listen to oral arguments presented to the Justices.

7. Where is the Korean War Veterans Memorial located?
   a. The Ellipse
   b. The Mall
   c. The Botanic Gardens
   d. Constitution Gardens

8. TRUE OR FALSE: The visitor's center in the Bureau of Engraving and Printing sells bags of shredded American currency as a souvenir.

9. What shape is the Ellipse?
   a. Square
   b. Triangular
   c. Round
   d. Pentagonal

10. What is the location of the proposed World War II Memorial?
    a. The Ellipse
    b. The Mall
    c. The Botanic Gardens
    d. Constitution Gardens

III

The American Military

QUIZ 15

The Branches
of the U.S. Military

☆ ☆ ☆ ☆ ☆

Answer the following questions about the United States' Army, Navy, Air Force, Marine Corps, and Coast Guard.

1. Name the highest achievable rank in each of the four branches of the U.S. military.

   Army _____

   Navy _____

   Air Force _____

   Marine Corps _____

2. Name the lowest rank in the four branches of the U.S. military.

   Army _____

   Navy _____

   Air Force _____

   Marine Corps _____

3. Match the number of total military personnel serving from the right column with the war in which they served from the left column.

   1. The Civil War–Union   a. 4,734,991

   2. World War I   b. 8,744,000

   3. World War II   c. 5,720,000

   4. Korean War   d. 2,213,363

   5. Vietnam War   e. 16,112,566

Marine uniforms

4. What year did President Nixon put an end to the military draft?

    a. 1972   c. 1974

    b. 1973   d. 1975

5. What are MREs?

6. On March 3, 1911 Congress authorized the first aviation appropriation for the Army, the beginning of the modern Air Force. What was the amount of this appropriation?

   a. $12,500

   b. $125,000

   c. $1,250,000

   d. $12,500,000

7. TRUE OR FALSE: In 1979, President Carter vetoed a pending defense bill because it included appropriations for a new nuclear aircraft carrier.

8. TRUE OR FALSE: The United States Marine Corps is a separate military service within the Department of the Navy and under the authority of the Secretary of the Navy.

9. The United States Army became a permanent military institution on June 3, 1784, when the Confederation Congress approved a resolution to establish a regiment of officers and men to protect the U.S. territories. What was the size of this first U.S. Army contingent?

   a. seven hundred

   b. one thousand

   c. fifteen thousand

   d. seventy thousand

10. Which federal department has direct command of the Coast Guard?

    a. The Department of the Treasury

    b. The Department of the Navy

    c. The Department of Transportation

    d. The Environmental Protection Agency

QUIZ 16

Military Milestones

☆ ☆ ☆ ☆ ☆

Match the date from the left column with the milestone in military history from the right column.

1. October 13, 1775

2. November 10, 1775

3. October 21, 1797

4. 1802

5. October 10, 1845

6. November 27, 1901

7. August 1, 1907

8. August 2, 1909

9. January 28, 1915

10. 1917

11. July 21, 1930

12. August 6, 1941

13. October 19, 1947

14. January 21, 1954

15. July 11, 1955

a. The United States Marine Corps is established.

b. Chuck Yeager breaks the sonic barrier in a Bell Aircraft X-1 research plane.

c. The Army War College is established.

d. The United States Congress approves drafting men aged twenty-one to thirty into the military.

e. The *Enola Gay* drops an atomic Bomb on Hiroshima, Japan.

f. The United States Air Force Academy is established.

g. The United States Army Air Force is established.

h. The United States Naval Academy is opened at Annapolis, Maryland.

i. "Old Ironsides"—the USS *Constitution* is launched.

j. The United States Navy is established.

k. The first atomic-powered submarine, the *Nautilus*, is launched.

l. The United States Coast Guard is established.

m. The United States buys the first military airplane from the Wright Brothers.

n. The United States Military Academy is established.

o. The United States Veterans Administration is established.

QUIZ 17

The Price of Freedom:
American Battle Deaths in Twelve Wars

We must never forget those Americans who have died in combat. Agreeing to put one's life on the line for one's country is the ultimate act of patriotism.

Match the war from the left column with the number of American dead from the right column.

CONFLICT

BATTLE DEATHS

1. The Revolutionary War (1775–1783)   a. 148

2. The War of 1812 (1812–1815)   b. 385

3. The Mexican War (1846–1848)   c. 919

4. The Civil War (1861–1865)   d. 1,020

5. The Indian Wars (1865–1898)   e. 1,733

6. The Spanish-American War (1898–1899)   f. 2,260

7. The Philippine War (1898–1902)   g. 6,824

8. World War I (1917–1918)   h. 33,746

9. World War II (1941–1945)   i. 47,355

10. The Korean War (1950–1953)   j. 53,402

11. The Vietnam War (1964–1973)   k. 214,938

12. The Persian Gulf War (1990–1991)   l. 291,557

IV

America
at War

The Revolutionary War

1. What was the span of the Revolutionary War?
   a. 1776–1777   c. 1774–1783
   b. 1775–1783   d. 1775–1776

2. On April 23, 1775, who made the following statement? "The colonies are in open and avowed rebellion. The die is now cast. The colonies must either submit or triumph."
   a. Benedict Arnold   c. Paul Revere
   b. Thomas Paine   d. King George III of Great Britain

3. Which U.S. military branch was established by the Continental Congress on November 28, 1775?
   a. Army   c. Air Force
   b. Navy   d. Marines

4. What was the name of the pamphlet written by Thomas Paine and published in January 1776 that explained the reasons the colonies should sever ties with England?

5. Who said the following? "Britain is the parent country, say some. Then the more shame upon her conduct. Even brutes do not devour their young, nor savages make war upon their families . . ."

6. TRUE OR FALSE: The U.S. Secret Service was formed during the Revolutionary War and placed under the command of Aaron Burr.

7. Where did George Washington and his troops spend the winter of 1777–1778?

   a. York, Pennsylvania

   b. Philadelphia, Pennsylvania

   c. Valley Forge, Pennsylvania

   d. New York City

8. What was Benedict Arnold's traitorous act?

   a. He plotted to assassinate George Washington for a British reward.

   b. Using U.S. supply wagons, he smuggled arms to British troops in New York.

   c. He conspired to turn West Point over to the British.

   d. He revealed U.S. troop movements to British commanders.

9. What was the name of the British commander who surrendered to George Washington at Yorktown in 1781, ending the Revolutionary War?

   a. Charles Cornwallis

   b. Friedrich Baum

   c. Henry Clinton

   d. William Howe

10. On September 3, 1783, a treaty was signed between Great Britain and the United States, officially ending the Revolutionary War. What was the name of this treaty?

QUIZ 19

American Revolution Battles

☆ ☆ ☆ ☆ ☆

Match the ten American Revolution battles from the left column with the date of the conflict from the right column.

1. The Battle at Lexington Green

2. The Battle at Bunker Hill

3. The American Invasion of Canada

4. The Battle of Valcour Island

5. Battles for New York

6. The Battle of Trenton

7. The Battle of Princeton

8. The Battle of Hubbardton

9. The Battle of Stony Point

10. The Seige of Yorktown

a. August 1775–October 1776

b. August 27–October 28, 1776

c. January 3, 1777

d. October 11–13, 1776

e. July 16, 1779

f. July 7, 1777

g. April 19, 1775

h. October 6–20, 1781

i. December 26, 1776

j. June 17, 1775

An American Revolution Timeline Quiz

☆ ☆ ☆ ☆ ☆

Match the American Revolution date from the left column with the American Revolution event from the right column.

1. April 1775

2. May 1775

3. June 1775

4. December 1775

5. April 1776

6. July 4, 1776

7. September 1776

8. October 1776

9. June 14, 1777

10. November 1977

11. February 1778

12. March 1778

13. October 1781

14. June 1782

15. November 1783

a. The Battle of Bunker Hill, the first major battle between American and British forces, is fought in Boston.

b. The American Navy is defeated by the British on Lake Champlain.

c. The Continental Congress, in defiance of King George's "no trade" proclamation, declares all American ports open to trade with every nation except England.

d. George Washington delivers his Farewell Address.

e. The British Army surrenders at Yorktown.

f. Massachusetts Governor Gage orders seven hundred British soldiers to destroy the American colonists' weapons depot on secret orders from the British.

g. The U.S. signs a treaty with France in which France agrees to fight for the colonies until their independence is won.

h. Congress adopts the Articles of Confederation.

i. Congress adopts the Great Seal of the United States.

j. Nathan Hale is executed by the British without a trial.

k. King George issues a proclamation closing off trade to the American colonies.

l. A British Parliament Peace Commission travels to Philadelphia where it agrees to grant all of the Americans' demands, except independence. Their offer is refused.

m. The United States declares its independence from England.

n. A thirteen-star, thirteen-stripe flag is legislated by Congress as the official flag of the United States.

o. The Second Continental Congress convenes in Philadelphia.

QUIZ 21

The War of 1812

☆ ☆ ☆ ☆ ☆

1. The U.S. fought _____ in the War of 1812.
   - a. Britain
   - b. France
   - c. Spain
   - d. Mexico

2. Which phrase has been used to describe the War of 1812?
   - a. The Merchant Sailors' War
   - b. The Battle of the Sea Lanes
   - c. The Second American War for Independence
   - d. The War on the Water

3. How long did the War of 1812 last, and in what year did it end?
   - a. One year, 1813
   - b. Two years, 1814
   - c. Three years, 1815
   - d. Four years, 1816

4. What was the cause of the War of 1812?
   - a. Benjamin Franklin's affair with a member of French royalty
   - b. A Spanish embargo of U.S. merchant ships
   - c. The assassination of a U.S. Senator
   - d. Violations of American shipping rights

5. TRUE OR FALSE: America invaded and occupied Canada during the War of 1812.

6. What famous Washington building was burned during the War of 1812?
   - a. Ford's Theater
   - b. The Library of Congress
   - c. The White House
   - d. The Supreme Court
   - e. The National Aquarium

7. Who was the American naval commander who won the Battle of Lake Erie in 1813 during the War of 1812?

   a. Matthew Perry   c. Charles Wilkes
   b. Oliver Perry   d. Robert Peary

8. Fill in the blanks in this quote from the War of 1812: "We have _____ the _____, and _____ are _____!"

9. The greatest victory for the Americans during the War of 1812 came in the Battle of New Orleans. Who was the American commanding general during this battle?

   a. Andrew Jackson   c. Zachary Taylor
   b. John Quincy Adams   d. James Polk

10. TRUE OR FALSE: The pivotal Battle of New Orleans was fought two weeks after the War of 1812 ended.

QUIZ 22

The Mexican War

1. When did the Mexican War take place?
   a. From 1812–1815
   b. From 1846–1848
   c. From 1901–1904
   d. America's war with Mexico is ongoing

2. TRUE OR FALSE: One of the reasons for the Mexican War was the U.S. annexation of Texas, which Mexico claimed as theirs.

3. Define "Manifest Destiny."

4. Who was President during the Mexican War?
   a. John Tyler
   b. Millard Fillmore
   c. Zachary Taylor
   d. James Polk

5. What was the size of Mexico's Army at the beginning of the Mexican War?
   a. 35,000
   b. 50,000
   c. 100,000
   d. 350,000

6. What was the size of the U.S. Army at the beginning of the Mexican War?
   a. 7,500
   b. 75,000
   c. 100,000
   d. 500,00

7. Which American writer, when writing about the Mexican War, said it was time for the world to see that "America knows how to crush, as well as how to expand"?
   a. Carl Sandburg
   b. Walt Whitman
   c. Edgar Allan Poe
   d. Mark Twain

8. TRUE OR FALSE: Henry David Thoreau went to jail rather than pay a tax that would be used to fund the Mexican War.

9. TRUE OR FALSE: During the Mexican War, 9,207 American soldiers deserted.

10. TRUE OR FALSE: At the end of the Mexican War, Mexico renounced all claims to Texas north of the Rio Grande.

BRAINBUSTER: What was the name of the Treaty that ended the Mexican War?
   a. The Treaty of Santa Anna
   b. The Treaty of San Jacinto
   c. The Treaty of Guadalupe Hidalgo
   d. The Rio Grande Treaty

QUIZ 23

The Civil War

☆ ☆ ☆ ☆ ☆

1. When did the Civil War take place?
   a. From 1851–1855
   b. From 1861–1865
   c. From 1871–1875
   d. From 1881–1885

2. TRUE OR FALSE: In the conflict, the southern states were known as the "Union."

3. TRUE OR FALSE: In the conflict, the northern states were known as the "Confederacy."

4. Which of the following is also used to describe the Civil War?
   a. The War for Southern Independence
   b. The War Between the States
   c. The Slaves' War
   d. The War for Equality

5. What was the first slave state to secede from the Union?
   a. Virginia
   b. Tennessee
   c. South Carolina
   d. Arkansas

6. TRUE OR FALSE: West Virginia was created by Virginians who refused to secede from the Union.

7. TRUE OR FALSE: Within months of the legal abolition of slavery, the Ku Klux Klan was founded in Pulaski, Tennessee.

8. Was the first shot fired in the Civil War fired from a Union weapon or a Confederate weapon?

9. Who captured, evacuated, and burned Atlanta, Georgia in the fall of 1864?

10. By what year were *all* the seceded Southern States readmitted to the United States?
    a. 1865
    b. 1866
    c. 1869
    d. 1870

QUIZ 24

Memorable Civil War Battles

☆ ☆ ☆ ☆ ☆

Match the ten Civil War battles from the left column with the date of the conflict from the right column.

1. Battle of McDowell, Virginia

2. Battle of Champion Hill, Mississippi

3. Battle of Fredericksburg, Virginia

4. Battle at Five Forks, Virginia

5. Battle of Kennesaw Mountain, Georgia

6. Battle of Spotsylvania Court House, Virginia

7. Battle of Chickamauga, Georgia

8. Battle of New Market, Virginia

9. The First Battle of Bull Run

10. The Battle of Shiloh

a. December 11–13, 1862

b. July 21, 1861

c. May 8, 1862

d. May 16, 1863

e. April 1, 1865

f. September 18–20, 1863

g. June 27, 1864

h. May 15, 1864

i. May 8–21, 1864

j. April 6–7, 1862

QUIZ 25

Civil War Firsts

☆ ☆ ☆ ☆ ☆

Match the Civil War first from the left column with its person, place, or thing from the right column.

1. This private received the first Congressional Medal of Honor.

2. This woman was the first female victim of the war.

3. This battle was the first in which black troops fought for the Union.

4. This was where the first shot was fired in defense of the Union.

5. This general was the first general to be replaced by President Lincoln during the war.

6. The first plantation mansion seized by Union forces belonged to this woman.

7. This was the first Indian tribe to declare its loyalty to the Confederacy.

a. Port Hudson, Louisiana, May 27, 1863

b. Pensacola, Florida

c. Burning Springs, Virginia

d. The Choctaws

e. Fort Donelson, Tennessee, February 13–16, 1862

f. Mrs. Judith Henry

g. Ulysses S. Grant

h. Colonel Ely Parker

i. Mrs. Robert E. Lee

j. Private Jacob Parott of the Andrews' Raiders

k. Irvin McDowell, replaced by General McClellan

l. Major Martin R. Delany

m. Richmond, Virginia

8. This man was the first black field officer.

9. This was the location of the first Confederate military prison.

10. The first military attack on an oil installation was made here.

11. The first time a railroad was used to transport troops was when Confederate soldiers were moved to this battle.

12. This man was the highest ranking civilian to volunteer for service during the Civil War.

13. This man was the first American Indian to serve as a military secretary to a commanding general.

14. This was where Union forces won their first major victory.

15. This man was the first to hold the rank of General of the Army.

n. Vice President Hannibal Hamlin

o. First Bull Run, July 18, 1861

QUIZ 26

The Spanish-American War

☆ ☆ ☆ ☆ ☆

1. Who was President during the Spanish-American War?
   a. Benjamin Harrison   c. William McKinley
   b. Grover Cleveland   d. Theodore Roosevelt

2. TRUE OR FALSE: The Rough Riders were an elite group of trained Marines.

3. During the Spanish-American War, the Rough Riders became famous for a victorious charge at the Battle of San Juan Hill in Cuba. Who led this charge?
   a. General Zachary Taylor   c. Admiral George Dewey
   b. Admiral Hyman Rickover   d. Colonel Theodore Roosevelt

4. The mysterious explosion of the U.S. battleship *Maine* spurred Congress to declare war on Spain. Where did the *Maine* explode?
   a. North of the Florida Keys
   b. In the harbor of Havana, Cuba
   c. In the harbor of San Juan, Puerto Rico
   d. Berthed at Miami

5. How many died in the explosion of the USS *Maine*?
   a. There were no fatalities in the explosion of the *Maine*.
   b. 16 of its crew of 354
   c. 266 of its crew of 354
   d. All of its crew of 354

6. TRUE OR FALSE: The explosion of the *Maine* was caused by an attack by a Spanish battleship.

7. How long was the Spanish-American War?
   a. 112 days
   b. 8 months
   c. 1 year
   d. 3 years

8. What was the name of the Treaty signed in December 1898 in which Spain gave up Cuba, the Philippines, Puerto Rico, and Guam?

9. At the conclusion of the Spanish-American War, how much did the United States pay to Spain for sovereignty rights to the Philippines?
   a. Nothing
   b. $1
   c. $1 million
   d. $20 million

10. What was the number of U.S. battle deaths in the Spanish-American War?
    a. Zero
    b. 10
    c. 385
    d. 3,102

World War I

☆ ☆ ☆ ☆ ☆

1. When did World War I take place?
   a. From 1904–1914
   b. From 1914–1917
   c. From 1914–1918
   d. From 1917–1918

2. Which of the following countries were members of the Allies?
   a. France
   b. Russia
   c. Germany
   d. Italy

3. What sparked the beginning of World War I?
   a. The election of Woodrow Wilson as President of the United States
   b. The assassination of Archduke Francis Ferdinand, heir to the throne of the Austrian Empire
   c. The sinking of the *Lusitania*
   d. The sinking of the *Titanic*

4. TRUE OR FALSE: A doughboy was a U.S. infantry soldier who fought during World War I.

5. What term was used to describe the dominant form of combat during World War I?
   a. Blitzkrieg warfare
   b. Guerilla warfare
   c. Germ warfare
   d. Trench warfare

6. In what year did the United States enter World War I?
   a. 1914
   b. 1915
   c. 1916
   d. 1917

7. What was the catalyst for the United States' entry into World War I?
   a. The sinking of the British passenger ship *Lusitania* by the Germans
   b. The assassination of Archduke Francis Ferdinand, heir to the throne of the Austrian Empire
   c. The shooting of eighteen American miners by Pancho Villa
   d. The suspicious explosion of a DuPont munitions plant in Wilmington, Delaware

8. How many Americans served during World War I?
   a. 4,734,991   c. 8,744,000
   b. 16,112,566   d. 467,159

9. What was the truly ironic slogan President Woodrow Wilson used during his second Presidential campaign?

10. What was the name of the Treaty that ended World War I?
    a. The Wilson Treaty
    b. The Fourteen Points Treaty
    c. The Treaty of Alsace-Lorraine
    d. The Treaty of Versailles

QUIZ 28

World War II

☆ ☆ ☆ ☆ ☆

A U.S. Navy destroyer during World War II

1. Which of the following were Axis powers during World War II?

    a. Italy

    b. Germany

    c. Japan

    d. France

2. Which of the following were Allied powers during World War II?

    a. Soviet Union

    b. United States

    c. France

    d. Britain

    e. All of the above

3. TRUE OR FALSE: World War II began when the Japanese bombed Pearl Harbor.

4. Who was Prime Minister of Britain during World War II?

5. TRUE OR FALSE: The Battle of the Bulge was the first major offensive by the German army during World War II.

6. TRUE OR FALSE: "V-E Day" marked the day the Allies were victorious over Japan during World War II.

7. TRUE OR FALSE: The Japanese refused to surrender after the United States dropped an atomic bomb on Hiroshima.

8. Fill in the blanks: "Yesterday, December _____, 1941— a _____ which will live in _____ —the United States of America was _____ and _____ attacked by _____ and _____ forces of the _____ of _____."

9. Who was President of the United States at the end of World War II?
   a. Franklin Delano Roosevelt   c. Herbert Hoover
   b. Harry Truman   d. Dwight D. Eisenhower

10. How many Americans served during World War II?
    a. 1,500,000   c. 8,744,000
    b. 5,720,000   d. 16,112,566

QUIZ 29

The Korean War

1. When did the Korean War take place?
   a. From 1950–1951
   c. From 1949–1955
   b. From 1950–1952
   d. From 1950–1953

2. What started the Korean War?
   a. North Korea executed a team of United Nations peacekeepers.
   b. China shot down an American plane bringing medical supplies to South Korea.
   c. South Korea invaded China.
   d. North Korea invaded South Korea.

3. TRUE OR FALSE: Officially, the combatants in the Korean War were North Korea and the United Nations.

4. TRUE OR FALSE: The majority of the troops that fought in the Korean War were South Korean, British, Canadian, and Australian.

5. Who was President of the United States during the Korean War?
   a. Franklin Delano Roosevelt
   c. Herbert Hoover
   b. Harry Truman
   d. Dwight D. Eisenhower

6. In the history of the Korean War, what is the significance of the names Thunderbolt, Roundup, Killer, Ripper, and Rugged?

7. Why was General Douglas MacArthur relieved of duty during the Korean War?

   a. He undermined Presidential prerogative by directly threatening the enemy with a belligerent broadcast ultimatum.

   b. By his actions, he confused allies and enemies about who was conducting the war.

   c. He directly challenged the President's authority as Commander in Chief.

   d. All of the above

8. How many American soldiers died in the Korean War?

   a. 3,476   c. 33,746

   b. 25,000   d. None

9. TRUE OR FALSE: The Korean War was the first time Mobile Army Surgical Hospitals (MASH) were used in the Far East Theater.

10. On Sunday, June 25, 1950, the President received the following phone call: "Mr. President, I have some very serious news. The North Koreans have invaded South Korea." Who made this phone call to the President?

    a. Secretary of State Dean Acheson

    b. Secretary of Defense Louis Johnson

    c. Vice President Alben Barkley

    d. General Douglas MacArthur

QUIZ 30

The Vietnam War

☆ ☆ ☆ ☆ ☆

The Vietnam Wall

1. Who said the following?

    "No event in American history is more misunderstood than the Vietnam War. It was misreported then, and it is misremembered now. Rarely have so many people been so wrong about so much. Never have the consequences of their misunderstanding been so tragic."

    a. Lyndon Johnson

    b. Richard Nixon

    c. General William C. Westmoreland

    d. Henry Kissinger

2. TRUE OR FALSE: Most Vietnam veterans were drafted.

3. TRUE OR FALSE: The fall of Saigon happened on April 30, 1975, two years *after* the American military left Vietnam.

4. TRUE OR FALSE: Kim Phuc, the little nine-year-old Vietnamese girl running naked from the napalm strike near Trang Bang on June 8, 1972, was burned by Americans bombing Trang Bang.

5. When did the Vietnam War take place?
   a. From 1954–1975
   b. From 1964–1973
   c. From 1954–1973
   d. From 1949–1979

6. What form of combat was commonplace during the Vietnam War?
   a. Blitzkrieg warfare
   b. Guerilla warfare
   c. Germ warfare
   d. Trench warfare

7. United States involvement in the Vietnam War spanned the administrations of four U.S. presidents. Name them.

8. Where is the Vietnam Memorial Wall?
   a. Dallas, Texas
   b. West Point
   c. Washington, D.C.
   d. Ho Chi Minh City, South Vietnam

9. Who negotiated the 1973 cease fire with North Vietnam?
   a. General William C. Westmoreland
   b. Richard Nixon
   c. Henry Kissinger
   d. General Barry McCaffrey

10. How many Vietnam veterans are severely disabled?
   a. Ten thousand
   b. Thirty-five thousand
   c. Fifty thousand
   d. Seventy-five thousand

The Persian Gulf War

☆ ☆ ☆ ☆ ☆

1. When did Saddam Hussein invade Kuwait?

   a. August 2, 1989

   c. August 2, 1991

   b. August 2, 1990

   d. August 2, 1992

2. TRUE OR FALSE: After Saddam Hussein invaded Kuwait, he declared it the nineteenth province of Iraq.

3. What was the purpose of Operation Desert Shield?

   a. To restore the Kuwaiti royal family to power

   b. To extinguish oil well fires in Kuwait

   c. To protect Saudi Arabia's oil fields from invasion by Saddam Hussein

   d. To invade Iran and depose the Ayatollah

4. TRUE OR FALSE: Following Saddam Hussein's invasion of Kuwait, the United Nations voted not to impose economic sanctions on Iraq.

5. On November 8th of that year, President Bush obtained a United Nations Security Council resolution against Iraq. What did the resolution mandate?

   a. It demanded that Iraq turn over Kuwaiti prisoners of war.

   b. It demanded that Saddam Hussein step down from power.

   c. It set a one-month deadline for Iraq to surrender to coalition forces.

   d. It set a January 15, 1991 deadline for Iraq to withdraw unconditionally from Kuwait.

An aircraft carrier has awesome size and power.

6. TRUE OR FALSE: The U.S. launched the most devastating air assault in history against military targets in Iraq and Kuwait.

7. How many American troops served in Kuwait?

8. What was the name of the military ground war offensive against Iraq in Kuwait?
   a. Operation Desert Storm   c. Operation Desert Fury
   b. Operation Sandstorm   d. Operation Tempest

9. TRUE OR FALSE: U.S. and coalition forces defeated Saddam Hussein's invading army in only four days.

10. What was the final act of destuction perpetrated by the retreating Iraqi army against Kuwaiti's infrastructure?
    a. They blew up every electrical substation they came upon.
    b. They set fire to over five hundred of Kuwait's oil wells.
    c. They poisoned every well in Kuwait.
    d. They destroyed every paved road they came upon.

V

The White House

QUIZ 32

The President's House

Answer the following questions about the White House:

1. TRUE OR FALSE: Before Washington, D.C., was decreed to be the seat of the federal Government in 1790, the U.S. Government resided temporarily in Philadelphia after moving from New York.

2. TRUE OR FALSE: The winning design for the White House was drawn by an Irish architect named James Hoban, who beat designs submitted by architect James Diamond and founder Thomas Jefferson, and who was awarded $500 for his work.

3. In 1814, during the War of 1812, the British set fire to the White House. What prevented the building from being completely consumed by flames?

4. TRUE OR FALSE: The Oval Office is in the East Wing.

5. During this President's tenure in the White House, electric lights were installed for the first time. The President was terrified of the light switches and thought that he would be zapped with electric shocks if he touched them. Thus, he left all the lights in the White House on all night long, rather than turn them off and risk electrocution. The White House electrician would have to turn them off when he arrived for work in the morning. Who was this anxious Chief Executive?

6. Which President once got stuck in a White House bathtub, resulting in the installation of an extra large tub in the residence?

The White House—fit for either a king or a President.

7. TRUE OR FALSE: Warren G. Harding once lost a complete set of White House china in a poker game.

8. Some of the rooms of the White House are named after colors. Which of the following is *not* a White House room designation?
   a. Green   c. Red
   b. Blue   d. Orange

9. TRUE OR FALSE: The White House is also the only private residence of a head of state that is open to the public, free of charge.

10. Fill in the blanks: Fill in the correct numbers in this statement about the White House. (The answers to this question can be found on www.whitehouse.gov, a site well worth your time. **Note:** The official White House web site has a ".**gov**" as its domain prefix. The address www.whitehouse.**com** takes you to a porn site.)

There are _____ rooms, _____ bathrooms, and _____ levels in the Residence. There are also _____ doors, _____ windows, _____ fireplaces, _____ staircases, and _____ elevators. The White House kitchen has _____ full-time chefs. The kitchen can serve as many as _____ guests and hors d'oeuvres to more than _____ people.

VI

American Inventions and Breakthroughs

QUIZ 33

American Inventors
and Inventions

☆ ☆ ☆ ☆ ☆

Match the American invention from the left column with the American inventor from the right column.

1. The Airplane   a. Richard Charles Drew

2. Alcoholics Anonymous   b. Will Kellogg

3. The Apgar Scale   c. Linus Yale

4. The Artificial Heart   d. Clarence Birdseye

5. The Blender   e. Ray Tomlinson

6. The Blood Bank   f. Margaret Knight

7. The Brassiere   g. Carlton Cole Magee

8. Cheerleading   h. John Lee Love

9. Condensed Milk   i. Jonas Salk

10. Corn Flakes   j. Richard James

11. The Crossword Puzzle   k. Edward Lowe

12. Cruise Control   l. Fred Waring

13. The Cylinder Lock   m. Bill Wilson

14. The Dewey Decimal System   n. Jim Wheeler

15. The Disposable Diaper   o. Bette Nesmith Graham

16. The Drive-In Theater	p. Earl Mitchell, Sr.
17. E-Mail	q. Charles Richter
18. The Fountain Pen	r. Sylvester Graham
19. Frozen Foods	s. Alvin J. Fellows
20. Geodesic Dome	t. Wilbur and Orville Wright
21. The Graham Cracker	u. Albert J. Parkhouse
22. The Grocery Bag	v. Christopher Latham Sholes
23. Instant Replay	w. Ralph Teetor
24. The Jacuzzi®	x. Arthur Wynne
25. Kevlar®	y. Thomas Peebler
26. Kitty Litter®	z. Virginia Apgar
27. Liquid Paper®	aa. Stephanie Kwolek
28. The Light Bulb	bb. Thomas Edison
29. The Moonpie®	cc. Frank Zamboni
30. Morse Code	dd. Marion O'Brien Donovan
31. The MRI	ee. Sylvan Goldman
32. The Parking Meter	ff. George Crum
33. The Pencil Sharpener	gg. Henry S. Parmalee
34. Pet Rock	hh. Whitcomb Judson
35. The Polio Vaccine	ii. Raymond Damadian
36. Popsicle	jj. Mary Andersen
37. Potato Chips	kk. Samuel Morse
38. Q-Tips®	ll. Richard Hollingshead, Jr.
39. The Richter Scale	mm. Buckminster Fuller
40. The Safety Pin	nn. Thomas Sullivan

41.	The Shopping Cart	oo.	Leo Gerstenzang
42.	Slinky®	pp.	Gail Borden
43.	The Sprinkler Head	qq.	Gary Dahl
44.	The Tape Measure	rr.	Walter Hunt
45.	The Tea Bag	ss.	Melvil Dewey
46.	The Typewriter	tt.	Mary Phelps Jacob
47.	Windshield Wipers	uu.	Frank Epperson
48.	The Wire Coat Hanger	vv.	Roy Jacuzzi
49.	The Zamboni®	ww.	Robert Jarvik
50.	The Zipper	xx.	Lewis Waterman

QUIZ 34

American Medical Breakthroughs

1. In 1776, Physician Benjamin Rush became the surgeon general of the Continental Army and founded the first _____ _____ at the Pennsylvania Hospital.

2. In 1784, _____ _____ invented the bifocal lens.

3. In 1803, the blood disease _____ was identified for the first time.

4. In 1841, teacher _____ set in motion efforts to reform treatment of the mentally ill, resulting in more humane state insane asylums.

5. In 1846, dentist William Morton, in collaboration with surgeon John Warren, first used _____ for anesthesia during surgery to remove a tumor from a patient's neck.

6. In 1847, the American Medical Association held its first meeting in _____.

7. In 1872, the first U.S. nursing school was established at Bellevue Hospital in _____ _____.

8. In 1884, Dr. Edward Trudeau opened the first _____ sanitarium in the Adirondack Mountains in New York.

9. In 1910, U. S. physician James Herrick identified the disease that would come to be called _____ _____ anemia.

10. In 1914, biochemist Edward Kendall isolated and identified the thyroid hormone thyroxin, which eventually led him to isolate the corticosteroid _____.

11. In 1926, bacteriologist Thomas Rivera created the science of _____ by successfully distinguishing between bacteria and viruses.

12. In 1929, Biochemist Edward Doisy isolated the female sex hormone _____.

13. In 1932, heart specialist H.S. Hyman invented the first cardiac _____.

14. In 1933, geneticist Thomas Morgan proved that chromosomes carry _____ traits.

15. In 1937, physician D.W. Murray introduced the anti-blood-clotting factor _____ into American medical practice.

16. In 1945, Grand Rapids, Michigan began adding _____ to their water supply to help prevent tooth decay.

17. The world's first successful open-heart surgery was performed in the U.S. in _____.

18. In 1955, endocrinologist Gregory Pincus developed the first effective _____ pill, a medical breakthrough that would change sexual mores for all time.

19. In 1968, cardiovascular surgeons Charles Dotter and Melvin Judkins developed _____, a method of opening up clogged arteries using a tiny balloon.

20. In 1989, the American developers of the drug _____, which dissolves blood clots in heart attack patients, were named inventors of the year.

QUIZ 35

American Scientific Breakthroughs

1. In 1780, _____ belts were used for the first time in an automated flour mill.

2. In 1790, the start of the Industrial Revolution in the United States was marked by the opening of the first working _____ mill.

3. In 1798, _____ _____ invented standardized jigs for mass production.

4. In 1830, the first magnetic observator in the United States was established in _____.

5. In 1843, Elias Howe, Jr. invented the interlocking-stitch _____ machine.

6. On May 24, 1844, Samuel Morse sent the first telegraph message. The telegraph went from Washington, D.C. to Baltimore and consisted of the sentence, "What hath _____ _____!"

7. In 1846, Professor Elias Loomis developed and published the first comprehensive _____ map.

8. In 1852, Elisha Otis patented the first safety _____.

9. In 1865, Linus Yale invented the cylinder _____.

10. In 1875, using research and prototypes of Antonio Meucci, Alexander Graham Bell claimed to invent the _____.

11. In 1877, using metal cylinders to imprint sound and play it back, Thomas Edison invented the _____.

12. In 1879, Thomas Edison developed the long-lasting incandescent _____ _____.

13. In 1881, astronomer Edward Barnard was the first to discover a _____ in a photograph.

14. In 1893, Henry _____ test-drove the first gas-powered motor vehicle.

15. In 1896, biologist Edmund Wilson identified the basic unit of all living things, the _____.

16. On October 7, 1913, the Ford Motor Company used the _____ line for the first time, building a complete car in one and one-half hours.

17. In 1925, Clarence Birdseye invented a process for _____-_____ food.

18. In 1929, astronomer Edwin Hubble confirmed that the universe is _____.

Thomas Edison. If not for Tom, we'd all be watching television by candlelight.

19. In 1935, seismologist Charles Richter developed the Richter Scale for measuring the magnitude of _____.

20. In 1940, nine-year-old Milton Sirotta originated the googol, which is a one followed by _____ zeroes.

21. In 1946, the world's first digital computer was built at _____ University.

22. In 1947, chemist Willard Libby invented _____ dating, used to date objects going back as far as 4300 B.C.

23. On October 14, 1947, Captain Charles Yeager made the first successful piloted _____ flight.

24. In December 1951, the first nuclear power reactor began generating electricity in _____.

25. In 1973, the _____ _____ system for pricing objects by scanning a series of lines is introduced.

American Religious Milestones

☆ ☆ ☆ ☆ ☆

Match the Supreme Court case from the left column with the religious issue it resolved from the right column.

1. *Lee v. Weisman* (1992)

2. *Walz v. Tax Commission* (1970)

3. *Reynolds v. United States* (1879)

4. *Cruz v. Beto* (1972)

5. *Wallace v. Jaffree* (1985)

6. *Bob Jones University v. United States* (1983)

7. *Thomas v. Review Board of the Indiana Employment Security Division* (1981)

8. *Lynch v. Donnelly* (1984)

9. *School District of Abington v. Schempp* (1963)

10. *Church of the Lukumi Babalu Aye v. City of Hialeah* (1993)

a. This case reaffirmed the exclusion of church properties from taxation.

b. This case ruled that prisoners have a right to practice their religion while incarcerated.

c. This case denied tax-exempt status to private schools that practiced racial discrimination.

d. This case ruled that a Seventh-Day Adventist woman who was fired for refusing to work on Sundays because of her religious beliefs was entitled to unemployment compensation benefits.

e. This case ruled that a city was not showing favoritism for one religion over another by allowing a Nativity scene to be displayed on public property.

f. This case expanded the Court's ban on school prayer to include Bible reading.

g. This case ruled that officially sanctioned prayer at public school graduation ceremonies violated the establishment clause of the First Amendment.

h. This case overturned a Florida law that banned the use of animals in religious rites, thereby allowing such use.

i. This case ruled that Alabama's "moment of silence" in school classrooms was a violation of the First Amendment.

j. This case ruled that polygamy was illegal, even though the Mormons claimed it was their religious right. This established that criminal or morally offensive acts conducted under the auspices of religion are not protected by the First Amendment.

VII

America in Space

QUIZ 37

The History of the U.S. Space Program

☆ ☆ ☆ ☆ ☆

1. Who was the physics professor who successfully launched the first liquid-propellant rocket?
   a. Dr. Robert Goddard
   b. Wernher von Braun
   c. John Glenn
   d. Edmund White

2. Where and in what year was the first liquid-propellant rocket launched?

3. In the 1940s and beyond, what kind of operations were carried out at the White Sands Proving Ground in New Mexico?
   a. The U.S. built enormous water tanks to simulate low- or no-gravity environments.
   b. The U.S. extensively studied recovered extraterrestrial spacecraft.
   c. The U.S. developed and tested larger rockets.
   d. Underground atomic testing

4. What year did the United States begin designing, developing, and building communications satellites?
   a. 1945
   b. 1955
   c. 1960
   d. 1965

5. TRUE OR FALSE: The first satellite successfully launched into orbit was American.

6. What was the United States' first manned space program?
   a. Project Gemini
   c. Project Mercury
   b. Project Apollo
   d. Project Atlas

7. What was the name of the United States' first space station?

8. Sixteen nations are contributing scientific expertise and resources to the construction and operation of the International Space Station. Name as many of these countries as you can.

9. How much did it cost to put a man on the moon?
   a. $500 million
   c. $10 billion
   b. $1 billion
   d. $25 billion

10. Fill in the blanks: "One small _____ for _____, one giant _____ for _____."

QUIZ 38

The Apollo Moon Missions

☆ ☆ ☆ ☆ ☆

Match the Apollo manned Moon Mission with the astronauts who flew it. (The mission's launch date is provided.)

1. *Apollo 8* (12/21/68)

2. *Apollo 10* (5/18/69)

3. *Apollo 11* (7/16/69)

4. *Apollo 12* (11/14/69)

5. *Apollo 13* (4/11/70)

6. *Apollo 14* (1/31/71)

7. *Apollo 15* (7/26/71)

8. *Apollo 16* (4/16/72)

9. *Apollo 17* (12/7/72)

a. Charles Conrad, Jr.; Richard F. Gordon; Alan L. Bean

b. Thomas P. Stafford; John W. Young; Eugene A. Cernan

c. Eugene A. Cernan; Ronald F. Evans; Harrison H. Schmitt

d. David R. Scott; Alfred M. Worden; James B. Irwin

e. Neil A. Armstrong; Michael Collins; Edwin "Buzz" Aldrin, Jr.

f. John W. Young; Thomas K. Mattingly II; Charles M. Duke, Jr.

g. Alan B. Shepherd, Jr.; Stuart A. Roosa; Edgar D. Mitchell

h. Frank Borman; James Lovell, Jr.; William A. Anders

i. James A. Lovell, Jr.; John L. Swiggert, Jr.; Fred W. Haise, Jr.

The Apollo Code
Names Quiz

☆ ☆ ☆ ☆ ☆

Match the Apollo mission from the left column with the code names
for its command/service and lunar modules from the right column.

1. *Apollo 9*

2. *Apollo 10*

3. *Apollo 11*

4. *Apollo 12*

5. *Apollo 13*

6. *Apollo 14*

7. *Apollo 15*

8. *Apollo 16*

9. *Apollo 17*

a. Command/Service Module
   Charlie Brown
   Lunar Module *Snoopy*

b. Command/Service Module
   Kitty Hawk
   Lunar Module *Antare*

c. Command/Service Module *America*
   Lunar Module *Challenger*

d. Command/Service Module *Casper*
   Lunar Module *Orion*

e. Command/Service Module
   Columbia
   Lunar Module *Eagle*

f. Command/Service Module *Endeavor*
   Lunar Module *Falcon*

g. Command/Service Module *Odyssey*
   Lunar Module *Aquarius*

A Lunar Lander. Say that one three times fast.

    h. Command/Service Module *Gumdrop*
       Lunar Module *Spider*

    i. Command/Service Module
       Yankee Clipper
       Lunar Module *Intrepid*

QUIZ 40

The Space Shuttle

☆ ☆ ☆ ☆ ☆

The space shuttle, pride of NASA

1. How long does it take the Space Shuttle to accelerate to a speed of seventeen thousand miles an hour after lift-off?

    a. Fifteen minutes   c. Ten minutes

    b. Twelve minutes   d. Eight minutes

2. TRUE OR FALSE: The Space Shuttle main engine delivers as much horsepower as nine locomotives.

3. According to NASA, how long would it take the turbopump on the Space Shuttle main engine to drain the average family-sized swimming pool?

    a. Ten minutes   c. One minute

    b. Five minutes   d. Twenty-five seconds

4. The Space Shuttle's three main engines and two solid rocket boosters generate _____ pounds of thrust at liftoff.

5. How cold is the liquid hydrogen in the Space Shuttle's main engine?
   a. −423 degrees Fahrenheit
   b. −42 degrees Fahrenheit
   c. Zero degrees Fahrenheit
   d. It isn't cold; it's the hottest substance on Earth.

6. How many Hoover Dams would it take to equal the energy released by the three Space Shuttle main engines?
   a. Two
   c. Twelve
   b. Five
   d. Twenty-three

7. TRUE OR FALSE: Each of the Shuttle's solid rocket motors burns five tons of propellant per second.

8. How tall is a stacked Space Shuttle booster?
   a. As tall as a two-story house
   b. As tall as the Washington Monument
   c. As tall as the Statue of Liberty
   d. As tall as the Sears Tower in Chicago

9. How many jumbo jets at takeoff would it take to equal the thrust of two Space Shuttle solid rocket motors?
   a. Ten jumbo jets
   c. Twenty-five jumbo jets
   b. Twenty jumbo jets
   d. Thirty-five jumbo jets

10. TRUE OR FALSE: Two Space Shuttle single rocket motors firing for two minutes produce enough energy to supply the entire power demand of eighty-seven thousand homes for a full day.

QUIZ 41

The Space Station

☆ ☆ ☆ ☆ ☆

1. TRUE OR FALSE: The Space Station is the largest manned object ever sent into space.

2. How many launches will it take to completely assemble the space station?
   a. Fifty-five—forty-one from the U.S. and fourteen from Russia
   b. Forty-five—thirty-six from the U.S. and nine from Russia
   c. Fifty—all from the U.S.
   d. One hundred—fifty from the U.S. and fifty from Russia

3. When the Space Station is fully built, how much of the world's population will be able to see it from the ground?
   a. Only people in the Northern hemisphere will be able to see it.
   b. Only people in the Southern hemisphere will be able to see it.
   c. Ninety percent of the world's population will be able to see it.
   d. Everyone on Earth will be able to see it.

4. Compared to living on Earth, do people living on the Space Station need more or less sleep?

5. TRUE OR FALSE: All of the hundreds of components of the Space Station will be assembled in space.

6. What will the astronauts aboard the Space Station spend the majority of their time doing?
   a. Exercising
   b. Sleeping
   c. Space walks
   d. Scientific experiments

7. How often does the Space Station circle the Earth?
   a. Every ten minutes
   b. Every ninety minutes
   c. Every three hours
   d. Once a day

8. How much exercise must the Space Station's astronauts do every day to prevent muscle wasting?
   a. Ten minutes
   b. Thirty minutes
   c. One hours
   d. Two hours

9. Sixteen nations are collaborating on the International Space Station. Name them.

10. TRUE OR FALSE: The Space Station is the most expensive single object ever built.

VIII

American Popular Culture

QUIZ 42

American Actors

☆ ☆ ☆ ☆ ☆

1. TRUE OR FALSE: Henry Fonda was the only juror to immediately vote "Guilty" in *12 Angry Men*.

2. An American actor who once played a mental patient with a taste for Juicy Fruit gum and baseball later played "President Dale" in the 1996 movie *Mars Attack!* Who is this actor?

3. Which of these American actors got his start on the TV series *Saturday Night Live*?
   a. Robin Williams
   b. John Travolta
   c. Matthew Broderick
   d. Chris Rock

4. This actor won a Best Actor Academy Award for his performance in *The Color of Money*. He made his film debut in the 1954 movie, *The Silver Chalice* in which he played a Greek sculptor who designed the chalice Jesus drank from at the Last Supper. The actor was so humiliated by this debut that he later ran an ad in *Variety* in which he actually apologized for the film. Who is this actor?

5. TRUE OR FALSE: Al Pacino dressed in drag as the soap opera character "Dorothy Michaels" in *Tootsie*.

6. Match the actor with their real name:

    1. John Wayne   a. Nicholas Coppola
    2. Edward G. Robinson   b. David Kominsky
    3. Nicolas Cage   c. Emmual Goldberg
    4. Danny Kaye   d. Marion Morrison
    5. Michael Landon   e. Eugene Orowitz

7. Who was a "Yankee Doodle Dandy?"

8. Fill in the blanks: Don Vito Corleone was played by _____
   _____.

9. TRUE OR FALSE: *Stalag 17* starred Robert Duvall as the sergeant suspected of being a Nazi spy.

10. Name the actor who wryly commented on a streaker's "shortcomings" at an Academy Award ceremony.

QUIZ 43

American Art and Artists

☆ ☆ ☆ ☆ ☆

Match the American artist from the left column with the art from the right column for which he or she is most well-known.

1. John James Audubon   a. Mobiles

2. Alexander Calder   b. Flowers and skulls

3. Homer Winslow   c. Drip paintings

4. Jasper Johns   d. Comic strips

5. Roy Lichtenstein   e. Dramatic watercolors

6. Georgia O'Keeffe   f. Campbell soup cans

7. Jackson Pollock   g. The Wild West

8. Frederic Remington   h. *Birds of America*

9. Andy Warhol   i. *American Gothic*

10. Grant Wood   j. Giant American flags and targets

QUIZ 44

American Best-Sellers of the Past Fifty Years

Answer these forty questions about best-selling books of the past fifty years. Some of the questions are detailed; some are no more than a couple of words. If you're a reader, these should not be that difficult.

1. This 1950 best-seller by Thor Heyerdahl told of the explorer's sea voyage from Peru to Easter Island.

2. This 1951 best-seller about Holden Caufield was the only novel published by its reclusive author.

3. This 1952 novel by John Steinbeck became a best-seller again in 2003 when Oprah picked it as the selection for her resurrected book club.

4. The sexual researcher who authored the groundbreaking 1953 best-seller, *Sexual Behavior in the Human Female*.

5. Norman Vincent Peale's 1954 best-seller touted the power of what?

6. This 1956 novel about sex scandals and nefarious schemers in a small New England town sold over ten million copies and was later made into a TV series.

7. This 1956 nonfiction best-seller was believed by many to prove the existence of reincarnation.

8. The title of this 1958 novel about an older man's obsession with a pre-teen girl is now a term used to describe a seductive adolescent girl.

9. This 1959 novel by D.H. Lawrence—the first full-text edition—had previously been published in an expurgated edition due to its sexual content.

10. This monumental study of Hitler's empire by William Shirer was a 1960 nonfiction best-seller.

11. This 1961 best-seller, first published in France in 1934, was the first book of a three-volume sexual autobiography by Henry Miller.

12. This somewhat scandalous 1962 nonfiction best-seller by Helen Gurley Brown proclaimed to the world that single girls had sex.

13. A 1964 best-seller by one of the Beatles.

14. This 1966 best-seller about drug use among well-off housewives was Jacqueline Susann's most famous success.

15. Truman Capote changed journalism with this 1966 best-seller about a multiple murder that he described as a "nonfiction novel."

16. Ira Levin's 1967 novel about a woman who gives birth to the son of Satan.

17. The story of the Corleones.

18. Jenny dies of leukemia.

19. This 1970 nonfiction best-seller was made into a movie by Woody Allen in which he played a reluctant sperm.

20. Pea soup vomit.

21. Richard Bach's 1972 bestseller, *Jonathan Livingston* _____.

22. Shark.

23. The Watergate book.

24. The 1977 sequel/prequel to *The Lord of the Rings*.

25. Kunta Kinte.

26. Cristina Crawford's 1978 literary dissection of her mother, Joan.

27. Stephen King's first best-seller.

28. Murdered doctor's 1979 diet book.

29. *When* _____ *Things Happen to* _____ *People.*

30. This 1982 best-seller sent men and women hunting for a particular spot guaranteed to trigger a female orgasm.

31. Sinatra sued to prevent the publication of this 1986 Kitty Kelley best-seller.

32. A 1988 best-seller by Stephen Hawking that many bought, but few may have actually read.

33. Salman Rushdie's 1989 best-seller that earned him a death sentence.

34. The authorized sequel to *Gone with the Wind.*

35. Conservative talk-show host Rush Limbaugh's first best-seller.

36. Madonna's porn photo book.

37. Howard Stern's *Private* _____.

38. *Men Are from* _____, *Women Are from* _____.

39. The 1996 roman à clef about Bill Clinton, initially released as by Anonymous.

40. The first Harry Potter book.

American Movies

☆ ☆ ☆ ☆ ☆

America's movies are the movies of the world. They are iconic touch-stones for generations of moviegoers in every country. This quiz exploits the familiarity everyone has with American movies. You will be given as brief a clue as possible; in some cases, no more than a single word. Your job is simple: Name that American movie!

1. Tara.

2. Corleone.

3. Bickle.

4. Dorothy.

5. Neff.

6. Shower.

7. "Phone home."

8. "Rosebud."

9. Clarice.

10. "Food fight!"

11. Alvy.

12. "I amuse you?"

13. "Adrian!"

14. Droogs.

15. Hal.

QUIZ 46

American Music

☆ ☆ ☆ ☆ ☆

1. TRUE OR FALSE: In the 1600s, the indigenous music in the Americas was the music of the American Indian.

2. TRUE OR FALSE: The music brought to the Americas from Europe during colonization was primarily religious in nature.

3. What was notable about William Billings's 1770 composition, "The New England Psalm Singer?"

   a. The lyrics were in Greek, when most musical compositions of the time were being written in Latin.

   b. Billings died immediately after writing the last note.

   c. It is believed to be the first American musical composition.

   d. Benjamin Franklin sent a copy of the piece to King George III.

4. The New York Metropolitan Opera gave its first performance in 1883. What opera was performed on this momentous occasion?

   a. Giuseppe's Verdi's *Rigoletto*

   b. Charles Gounod's *Faust*

   c. Gioacchino Rossini's *The Barber of Seville*

   d. Wolfgang Mozart's *The Marriage of Figaro*

5. What American composer wrote *Babes in Toyland*, one of the first American operettas?

   a. Victor Herbert   c. George Gershwin

   b. Charles Ives   d. Aaron Copland

6. Fill in the blank: *An American in* _____.

7. TRUE OR FALSE: American avant-garde composer John Cage once composed a piece called *Imaginary Landscape No. 4*, which consisted of twelve radios randomly tuned all at the same time.

8. What American composer wrote *West Side Story?*

9. Fill in the blank: *Appalachian* _____.

10. Fill in the blanks: Philip _____ wrote the modern opera, _____ *on the Beach.*

QUIZ 47

American Sports

☆ ☆ ☆ ☆ ☆

Special thanks to Mike Lewis for his contributions to this quiz. (Actually, the word should be "contribution" since I know less than nothing about sports and my colleague and cohort Mike took pity on me and wrote the entire quiz himself!)

1. Who was the goalie of the U.S. Ice Hockey team that won the gold medal by beating the Russians in the 1980 Winter Olympics in Lake Placid, New York?
   a. Jim Craig
   b. Mike Eruzione
   c. Herb Brooks
   d. Bruce Sutter

2. What did Cal Ripken, Jr. of the Baltimore Orioles do on September 20, 1998?

3. Who came up with the idea of the Super Bowl and when was the first game played?

4. In what year did Tiger Woods turn pro, and how old was he?

5. Match the NASCAR driver with his car number:
   1. 6
   2. 3
   3. 24
   4. 43
   a. Dale Earnhardt
   b. Jeff Gordon
   c. Richard Petty
   d. Mark Martin

6. By what name is soccer great Edson Arantes do Nascimento best known?
   a. Eddie
   b. Sulu
   c. Pelé
   d. Doug

7. What is the oldest major league baseball stadium?

   a. Wrigley Field   c. Yankee Stadium

   b. Shea Stadium   d. Fenway Park

8. TRUE OR FALSE: George W. Bush was at the controls of one of three F-16s that flew over Yankee Stadium during game one of the 2001 World Series.

9. What rushing record did OJ Simpson hold for eleven years?

10. Which of the following was *not* a Triple Crown winner?

    a. Seattle Slew   c. War Admiral

    b. Cigar   d. Affirmed

11. Mary Lou Retton won the all-around gold medal in what Olympic sports?

    a. Archery   c. Tennis

    b. Gymnastics   d. Downhill skiing

12. Mark Spitz was:

    a. A gold-medal winning swimmer

    b. A professional wrestler

    c. A jockey

    d. A cornerback for the Cleveland Browns

13. How many NBA championships did Michael Jordan win?

14. Who was Cy Young and what does he have to do with baseball today?

15. Which of these is NOT a current football team?

    a. Cleveland Browns

    b. Los Angeles Rams

    c. Houston Texans

    d. New Orleans Saints

16. TRUE OR FALSE: No one player has ever scored one hundred points in an NBA basketball game.

17. For what NBA team did Shaquille O'Neal initially play?

18. In football, what is the Neutral Zone?

19. Fill in the blanks: Complete this sentence from one of baseball's greatest speeches: "_____, I consider _____ the _____ man on the face of the _____."

20. Who holds the record for most consecutive baseball games with a hit, and when was the record set?

QUIZ 48

American TV

☆ ☆ ☆ ☆ ☆

1. Which American singer was shown on *The Ed Sullivan Show* only from his waist up because of his "obscene" hip movements?
   a. Bobby Darin
   b. Elvis Presley
   c. Little Richard
   d. Jerry Lee Lewis

2. How many sons did Steve Douglas have?
   a. One
   b. Two
   c. Three
   d. Four

3. TRUE OR FALSE: The longest running Western on network TV was *Bonanza*.

4. Fill in the blanks: Lucy and Ricky's landlords were _____ and _____ Mertz.

5. Who were the first two *60 Minutes* correspondents?
   a. Diane Sawyer and Harry Reasoner
   b. Dan Rather and Mike Wallace
   c. Morley Safer and Mike Wallace
   d. Mike Wallace and Harry Reasoner

6. On Dallas, what did the "J.R." in "J.R. Ewing" stand for?

7. Fill in the blanks:

There is nothing wrong with your _____ _____. Do not attempt to adjust the _____. We are controlling _____. We will control the _____. We will control the _____. We can change the focus to a _____ blur—or sharpen it to _____ clarity. For the next _____, sit quietly and we will _____ all that you _____ and _____. You are about to _____ in a great _____. You are about to experience the awe and _____ which reaches from the inner _____ to . . . the _____ *Limits*.

8. What did Ed Norton do for a living?
   a. He was a sewer worker.   c. He was a janitor.
   b. He drove a bus.   d. He was a doctor.

9. TRUE OR FALSE: Mr. Spock's "V" hand sign meant "Seek Victory over Klingons."

10. Which of the following is not a successful HBO series?
    a. *The Sopranos*   d. *The Wire*
    b. *Six Feet Under*   e. *Oz*
    c. *Sex and the City*   f. *Ally McBeal*

QUIZ 49

American Writers and Poets

☆ ☆ ☆ ☆ ☆

This is a *very difficult* American literature quiz that will probably require you to do some digging if you hope to complete it. Match the American writer from the left column with his or her work from the right column. Good luck and happy reading!

1. William Bradford

2. Anne Bradstreet

3. Samuel Sewall

4. Edward Taylor

5. Cotton Mather

6. Jonathan Edwards

7. Sarah Kemble Knight

8. William Byrd

9. John Woolman

10. St. Jean De Crevecoeur

11. Benjamin Franklin

12. Thomas Paine

13. Thomas Jefferson

14. Philip Freneau

15. Washington Irving

a. "Upon a Spider Catching a Fly"

b. "The Chambered Nautilus"

c. *Dark Laughter*

d. "Considerations on the True Harmony of Mankind on Merchandising"

e. *Walden*

f. "A White Heron"

g. "The Will to Believe"

h. "Sinners in the Hand of An Angry God"

i. "Charleston"

j. *Ethan Frome*

k. "Speech at Cooper Union"

l. "Roan Stallion"

16. James Fenimore Cooper

17. William Cullen Bryant

18. Nathaniel Hawthorne

19. Edgar Allan Poe

20. Herman Melville

21. Ralph Waldo Emerson

22. Henry David Thoreau

23. Henry Wadsworth Longfellow

24. John Greenleaf Whittier

25. Oliver Wendell Holmes

26. James Russell Lowell

27. Henry Timrod

28. Abraham Lincoln

29. Walt Whitman

30. Mark Twain

31. Bret Harte

32. George Washington Cable

33. Joel Chandler Harris

34. Sarah Orne Jewett

35. William Dean Howells

36. Henry James

37. Henry Adams

38. William James

39. William Vaughn Moody

m. *Of Plymouth Plantation*

n. *Happy Days*

o. *Cannery Row*

p. "You, Andrew Marvell"

q. "Telling the Bees"

r. "The Jilting of Granny Weatherall"

s. "The Topaz Cufflinks Mystery"

t. "The Short Happy Life of Francis Macomber"

u. *Flappers and Philosophers*

v. *The Journal of Madam Knight*

w. "Somewhere I Have Never Travelled, Gladly Beyond"

x. "The Coliseum"

y. "The Cathedral"

z. "The Yellow Violet"

aa. "The Indian Burying Ground"

bb. "The Flesh and the Spirit"

cc. "The Angelus"

dd. *Common Sense*

ee. "Justice Denied in Massachusetts"

ff. "Hugh Selwyn Mauberley"

40. Edith Wharton

41. Hamlin Garland

42. Stephen Crane

43. Theodore Dreiser

44. Edward Arlington Robinson

45. Robert Frost

46. Carl Sandburg

47. Willa Cather

48. Ellen Glasgow

49. H. L. Mencken

50. Sherwood Anderson

51. Sinclair Lewis

52. F. Scott Fitzgerald

53. Edna St. Vincent Millay

54. Eugene O'Neill

55. Ezra Pound

56. T. S. Eliot

57. Robinson Jeffers

58. Archibald MacLeish

59. Hart Crane

60. Katherine Anne Porter

61. William Faulkner

62. Ernest Hemingway

63. Thomas Wolfe

gg. "Rappaccini's Daughter"

hh. "Royal Palm"

ii. *Heart's Needle*

jj. *A Progress to the Mines*

kk. "Morning Hymn to a Dark Girl"

ll. "Editha"

mm. "Bartleby the Scrivener"

nn. *Henderson the Rain King*

oo. "Richard Cory"

pp. "Gloucester Moors"

qq. "The Return of a Private"

rr. *Leaves of Grass*

ss. "Notes on the State of Virginia"

tt. "The Over-Soul"

uu. *The Education of Henry Adams*

vv. "Jordan's End"

ww. *The Sketch Book*

xx. "Grass"

yy. "An Egyptian Pulled Glass Bottle in the Shape of a Fish"

zz. "The Man That Corrupted Hadleyburg"

64. John Steinbeck

65. Wallace Stevens

66. William Carlos Williams

67. Marianne Moore

68. John Crowe Ransom

69. e.e. cummings

70. John Dos Passos

71. James T. Farrell

72. James Thurber

73. Richard Eberhart

74. Theodore Roethke

75. Muriel Rukeyser

76. Robert Lowell

77. Richard Wilbur

78. Bernard Malamud

79. Flannery O'Connor

80. John Updike

81. Lawrence Ferlinghetti

82. Howard Nemerov

83. Denise Levertov

84. W. D. Snodgrass

85. James Wright

86. W. S. Merwin

87. Anne Sexton

aaa. *Letters From an American Farmer*

bbb. *Long Day's Journey Into Night*

ccc. "The Fastest Runner on Sixty-first Street"

ddd. "To Those Who Stand Upon the New Earth"

eee. "Only the Dead Know Brooklyn"

fff. "The Emperor of Ice-Cream"

ggg. "The Equilibrists"

hhh. *Manhattan Transfer*

iii. *An American Tragedy*

jjj. "Belles Demoiselles Plantation"

kkk. "The Sculptor's Funeral"

lll. *Absalom, Absalom!*

mmm. *The Red Badge of Courage*

nnn. "This is Just to Say"

ooo. "The Love Song of J. Alfred Prufrock"

ppp. *The Aspern Papers*

qqq. "You Know How Women Are"

88. Adrienne Rich	rrr. *The Deerslayer*
89. Sylvia Plath	sss. *Uncle Remus: His Songs and His Sayings*
90. LeRoi Jones	
91. Louis May Alcott	ttt. "Stopping by Woods on a Snowy Evening"
92. John Barth	uuu. "Opportunities to Do Good"
93. Saul Bellow	
94. Truman Capote	vvv. "The Jewish Cemetery at Newport"
95. John Cheever	
96. Pearl Buck	www. "The Speech of Polly Baker"
97. Jack Kerouac	xxx. "Santa Claus"
98. Erica Jong	yyy. *Little Men*
99. Thomas Harris	zzz. "For Theodore Roethke"
100. George Beahm	aaaa. "The Drunk in the Furnace"
101. Stephen King	
	bbbb. *Hannibal*
	cccc. *Fear of Flying*
	dddd. "My Papa's Waltz"
	eeee. *War of Words*
	ffff. "The Truth the Dead Know"
	gggg. "A Coney Island of the Mind"
	hhhh. *It*
	iiii. "The Third Dimension"
	jjjj. *Giles Goat-Boy*

kkkk. "In Memory of Radio"

llll. *The Natural*

mmmm. *Rabbit, Run*

nnnn. *On the Road*

oooo. *In Cold Blood*

pppp. *The Bell Jar*

qqqq. *The Good Earth*

rrrr. "Boy with His Hair Cut Short"

ssss. "Museum Piece"

tttt. "The Diamond Cutters"

uuuu. "The Life You Save May Be Your Own"

vvvv. *The Wapshot Chronicle*

wwww. "Rumination"

IX

American Holidays

QUIZ 50

Independence Day

☆ ☆ ☆ ☆ ☆

1. TRUE OR FALSE: Independence Day celebrates the signing of the Declaration of Independence.

2. Where was the Declaration of Independences signed?
   a. Boston, Massachusetts   c. Albany, New York
   b. Philadelphia, Pennsylvania   d. New York, New York

3. How many American colonies existed at the time of the signing of the Declaration of Independence?

4. TRUE OR FALSE: All the signers of the Declaration of Independence signed the document on July 4, 1776.

5. What was the dominant reason the colonies declared their independence from Britain?
   a. British troops occupied every public building.
   b. King George had insulted Martha Washington.
   c. No taxation without representation.
   d. British ships took every berth in all of the colonial harbors.

6. Why did John Hancock sign his name so large on the Declaration of Independence?

7. What was the first newspaper to print the Declaration of Independence for all to read?
   a. *Pennsylvania Evening Post*   c. *The Hartford Courant*
   b. *The New York Times*   d. *New York Post*

8. TRUE OR FALSE: The first public reading of the Declaration of Independence took place on July 8, 1776 in Philadelphia's Independence Square.

9. During the first public reading of the Declaration of Independence, a bell known as the Province Bell was tolled. What was the name of the Province Bell changed to after the reading of the Declaration of Independence?

10. Which of the following are associated with America's celebration of Independence Day?

    a. Fireworks   c. Picnics
    b. Parades   d. All of the above

QUIZ 51

Memorial Day

☆ ☆ ☆ ☆ ☆

1. What was the original name of the Memorial Holiday?
   a. Remembrance Day
   b. Decoration Day
   c. Honor Day
   d. Veterans' Respect Day

2. In 1966, who declared Waterloo, New York the official birthplace of the Memorial Day holiday?
   a. Lyndon Johnson
   b. The House of Representatives
   c. The Senate
   d. Richard Nixon

3. TRUE OR FALSE: Memorial Day was first observed on May 30, 1868, when flowers were placed on the graves of Civil War soldiers at Arlington National Cemetery.

4. What was the first state to officially recognize the Memorial Day holiday?
   a. Oregon
   b. Connecticut
   c. New York
   d. Texas

5. What year did the first American state officially recognize the Memorial Day holiday?
   a. 1888
   b. 1875
   c. 1890
   d. 1873

6. TRUE OR FALSE: By 1890, Memorial Day was recognized and observed by all the American states.

7. TRUE OR FALSE: The South refused to honor Memorial Day until after World War I.

8. TRUE OR FALSE: Congress passed a bill in 1971 mandating that Memorial Day was to be observed on the last Monday in May.

9. What flower is associated with Memorial Day?
   a. Daisy   c. White carnation
   b. Yellow rose   d. Red poppy

10. TRUE OR FALSE: There is currently a bill in Congress to move the Memorial Day holiday to May 30th.

QUIZ 52

Labor Day

☆ ☆ ☆ ☆ ☆

1. Who said the following:

   "Labor Day differs in every essential way from the other holidays of the year in any country. All other holidays are in a more or less degree connected with conflicts and battles of man's prowess over man, of strife and discord for greed and power, of glories achieved by one nation over another. Labor Day . . . is devoted to no man, living or dead, to no sect, race, or nation."

2. When is Labor Day celebrated?
   a. The second Monday in October
   b. The first Monday in September
   c. The second Monday in September
   d. The first Monday in October

3. TRUE OR FALSE: The first Labor Day holiday was celebrated on Tuesday, September 5, 1882, in New York City.

4. What was the name of the organization that proposed the first Labor Day observance?
   a. The Southern Labor Union
   b. The Eastern Labor Brotherhood
   c. The Central Labor Union
   d. The Northeast Brotherhood of Machinists

5. In what year was an official day for Labor Day decided upon?
   a. 1881   c. 1883
   b. 1882   d. 1884

6. What state was the first to propose Labor Day legislation?

   a. Oregon   c. Pennsylvania

   b. New York   d. New Jersey

7. What state was the first to pass a Labor Day celebration law?

   a. Oregon   c. Pennsylvania

   b. New York   d. New Jersey

8. TRUE OR FALSE: To join the states in celebrating Labor Day, Congress passed a law in 1894 decreeing it a legal U.S. holiday in the District of Columbia and the territories.

9. Which of the following are associated with Labor Day celebrations in the United States?

   a. Picnics   c. Sales

   b. Parades   d. All of the above

10. What is the Sunday before Labor Day known as?

QUIZ 53

Thanksgiving

☆ ☆ ☆ ☆ ☆

1. The Thanksgiving celebration generally considered to be the first in America took place in 1621, the fall after the *Mayflower* pilgrims arrived at _____.
   a. New Haven, Connecticut
   b. New Bedford, Massachusetts
   c. Plymouth Rock, Massachusetts
   d. Watch Hill, Rhode Island

2. TRUE OR FALSE: The first officially proclaimed Thanksgiving Day in America was June 29, 1676. The governing council of Charlestown, Massachusetts issued a proclamation.

3. Which of the following is *not* considered part of a traditional Thanksgiving dinner?
   a. Turkey   c. Pumpkin Pie
   b. Cranberry sauce   d. Ravioli

4. Who was Edward Rawson?
   a. The Charleston, Massachusetts clerk who was given the task of proclaiming June 29, 1676 as a day of thanksgiving
   b. The Charleston, Massachusetts tanner who was placed in the stocks for refusing to cease work on the first Thanksgiving
   c. The *Mayflower* sailor who first set foot on American soil
   d. The Plymouth, Massachusetts mayor who signed the first Thanksgiving proclamation.

5. In what year did the first Thanksgiving set in November take place?
   a. 1788   c. 1790
   b. 1789   d. 1801

6. Who signed the first federal proclamation setting aside a day in November as a day of thanksgiving and prayer?
   a. Roger Sherman   c. John Adams
   b. Thomas Jefferson   d. George Washington

7. TRUE OR FALSE: Almost one hundred Indians joined the Pilgrims for the first Thanksgiving celebration.

8. TRUE OR FALSE: The Thanksgiving celebrations of the 1700s were marked by great amounts of food and drink, dancing, and general revelry.

9. In 1863, President Lincoln issued a proclamation making the fourth Thursday in November Thanksgiving Day. This was changed in 1939 to the third Thursday in November to boost the economy and extend the Christmas shopping season. Who made the change?
   a. Herbert Hoover   c. Franklin Delano Roosevelt
   b. Calvin Coolidge   d. Harry Truman

10. Why was Thanksgiving officially changed in 1941 back to the fourth Thursday in November?
    a. Public protest
    b. So that it would occur on the vernal equinox
    c. To give farmers a longer period to get their final corn harvest into the stores
    d. Because the First Lady wanted it at the end of the month instead of during the third week

X

Great American Documents

QUIZ 54

The Articles
of Confederation

1. TRUE OR FALSE: The Articles of Confederation were drafted by the Continental Congress in 1781.

2. How many states ratified the Articles of Confederation?

3. Name the states that ratified the Articles of Confederation.

4. What was the last state to ratify the Articles of Confederation?
   a. Connecticut
   b. New York
   c. Massachusetts
   d. Maryland

5. What was the official name Congress adopted after the Articles of Confederation were ratified?
   a. The Congress of the States
   b. The United Congress
   c. The United States in Congress Assembled
   d. The United States Congress

6. Who was the first President of the new Congress?
   a. Samuel Huntington
   b. John Hancock
   c. Roger Sherman
   d. Thomas Jefferson

7. TRUE OR FALSE: The Articles of Confederation established the office of President of the United States.

8. TRUE OR FALSE: The Articles of Confederation included a provision for the federal government to collect personal taxes from citizens.

9. What term did the authors of the Articles of Confederation use to describe God?
   a. The Father of Mankind
   b. The Wondrous Lord of Creation
   c. The Lord of All
   d. The Great Governor of the World

10. What superseded the Articles of Confederation?

QUIZ 55

The Declaration of Independence

✩ ✩ ✩ ✩ ✩

**Sign on the dotted line: the founding fathers
draft the Declaration of Independence.**

1. Fill in the missing words from the opening paragraph of the Declaration of Independence.

   When in the _____ of _____ events, it becomes necessary for one _____ to _____ the political _____ which have _____ them with _____, and to assume among the _____ of the _____, the _____ and _____ station to which the _____ of _____ and of nature's _____ entitle them, a _____ respect to the _____ of _____ requires that they should _____ the _____ which impel them to the _____.

2. Which of the following are the "certain inalienable rights" claimed in the Declaration of Independence?

   a. Life   d. The pursuit of happiness

   b. Liberty   e. Free speech

   c. The right to vote

3. TRUE OR FALSE: One of the complaints against King George in the Declaration of Independence was that he allowed his officers to harass colonists and eat their food.

4. TRUE OR FALSE: One of the complaints against King George in the Declaration of Independence was that he made the British military independent of and superior to any and all civil authority in the Colonies.

5. How many men signed the Declaration of Independence?

6. What was the occupation of the majority of the signers of the Declaration of Independence?

7. On what date was the Declaration of Independence adopted?

8. Who wrote the Declaration of Independence?

9. The colonists had long tried to assert their independence by working within the confines of the British constitution. When this ultimately failed, they instead asserted their right to freedom by citing what?

10. The original draft of the Declaration of Independence charged King George with allowing the "cruel" slave trade to continue. Why was this accusation ultimately deleted by Congress?

QUIZ 56

The Constitution

☆ ☆ ☆ ☆ ☆

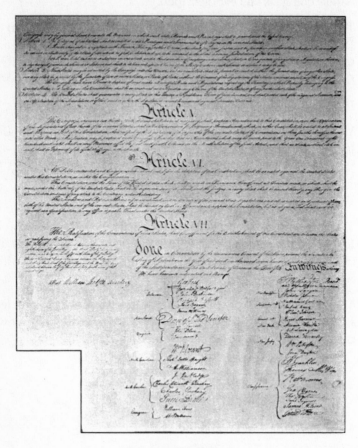

The U.S. Constitution

Answer the following questions about the world's first written Constitution and the document that sets the standard for all nations aspiring to liberty and democracy.

1. Fill in the missing words from the Preamble to the United States Constitution.

   We the _____ of the United States, in Order to form a more perfect _____, establish _____, insure domestic _____, provide for the common _____, promote the general _____, and secure the _____ of Liberty to ourselves and our _____, do _____ and _____ this _____ for the United States of America.

2. According to the Constitution, what is the name of the body made up of the Senate and the House of Representatives?

3. According to the Constitution, how old must a person be before he or she can be elected to the House of Representatives?

4. According to the Constitution, how many Senators are allowed to represent each state in the Union?

5. According to the Constitution, how old must a person be before he or she can be elected to the Senate?

6. TRUE OR FALSE: The Constitution gives Congress the power to collect taxes.

7. TRUE OR FALSE: Only the President of the United States can declare war.

8. TRUE OR FALSE: According to the Constitution, States can implement treaties and coin money.

9. TRUE OR FALSE: You are thirty-six years old, an American citizen, and have lived in Italy for the past twenty years. You decide to return to America and run for the office of U.S. President and the Constitution allows you to do so.

10. According to the Constitution, how often is the President obligated to report on the State of the Union?

11. Name the three reasons for which a President, Vice President, or other civil Officer of the United States may be impeached.

12. TRUE OR FALSE: The Supreme Court justices may willingly take a pay cut at any time.

13. According to the Constitution, how many witnesses are required to convict a person of Treason?

14. TRUE OR FALSE: A new state can legally and constitutionally be created inside the boundaries of an existing state.

15. TRUE OR FALSE: George Washington signed the United States Constitution.

QUIZ 57

The Bill of Rights

Fill in the missing words from the first ten amendments to the U.S. Constitution.

ARTICLE I

Congress shall make no _____ respecting an establishment of _____, or prohibiting the free exercise thereof; or abridging the freedom of _____, or of the _____; or of the right of the _____ peaceably to _____, and to _____ the _____ for a redress of _____.

ARTICLE II

A well-regulated _____, being necessary to the _____ of a free _____, the right of the people to keep and bear _____, shall not be _____.

ARTICLE III

No _____ shall, in time of _____ be quartered in any _____, without the _____ of the _____, nor in time of _____, but in a _____ prescribed by _____.

ARTICLE IV

The _____ of the people to be _____ in their _____,
houses, _____, and effects, against unreasonable _____ and
_____, shall not be violated, and no _____ shall issue, but
upon _____ _____, supported by oath or _____, and particularly
describing the _____ to be _____, and the _____ or
_____ to be _____.

ARTICLE V

No person shall be held to _____ for a _____, or otherwise
_____ crime, unless on a presentment or _____ of a _____
_____, except in cases arising in the _____ or _____ forces,
or in the _____, when in actual _____ in time of _____
or _____ _____; nor shall any _____ be _____ for the same
_____ to be _____ put in _____ of life or _____;
nor shall be compelled in any _____ case to be a _____
against _____, nor be _____ of life, _____, or property,
without due _____ of law; nor shall _____ property be taken
for _____ use, without just _____.

ARTICLE VI

In all criminal _____, the _____ shall enjoy the right to a
_____ and _____ trial, by an impartial _____ of the
State and district wherein the _____ shall have been _____,
which _____ shall have been previously ascertained by
_____, and to be _____ of the _____ and cause of
the _____; to be _____ with the _____ against him; to
have _____ process for obtaining _____ in his favor, and
to have the assistance of _____ for his _____.

ARTICLE VII

In suits at _____ law, where the _____ in _____ shall exceed _____ dollars, the right of _____ by _____ shall be _____, and no _____ tried by a _____, shall be otherwise _____ in any Court of the _____ _____, than according to _____ of common _____.

ARTICLE VIII

Excessive _____ shall not be required, nor excessive _____ imposed, nor _____ and _____ punishments inflicted.

ARTICLE IX

The enumeration in the _____, of certain _____, shall not be construed to _____ or _____ others retained by the _____.

ARTICLE X

The _____ not delegated to the _____ States by the _____, nor _____ by it to the _____, are reserved to the _____ respectively, or to the _____.

QUIZ 58

The Amendments

☆ ☆ ☆ ☆ ☆

This quiz covers the eleventh through twenty-seventh amendments to the United States Constitution. (See the quiz on the Bill of Rights for questions on the first ten amendments.)

1. The Thirteenth Amendment, ratified on December 6, 1865, prohibited slavery or involuntary servitude. Only one state of the existing thirty-six states refused to ratify this amendment. Name the state.

2. The Fifteenth Amendment, ratified on February 3, 1870, gave blacks and former slaves the right to vote. Only one state of the existing thirty-seven states refused to ratify this amendment. Name the state.

3. TRUE OR FALSE: The Sixteenth Amendment, ratified on February 3, 1913, gave Congress the power to impose a tax on income, no matter what the source of the income.

4. The Eighteenth Amendment is the only constitutional amendment ever to be repealed. What was the subject of the Eighteenth Amendment?

5. Which amendment repealed the Eighteenth Amendment?

6. TRUE OR FALSE: The Nineteenth Amendment gave women the right to vote.

7. According to the Twentieth Amendment, what happens if a President-elect dies before he is officially sworn in as President?

8. TRUE OR FALSE: Regardless of the media talk about former President Bill Clinton possibly running for a third term as President, the Twenty-second Amendment clearly forbids his election to a third term.

9. The Twenty-fourth Amendment, ratified on January 23, 1964, prohibited denying anyone the right to vote for failing to pay a poll tax or any other type of voting tax. Only one state of the existing fifty states refused to ratify this amendment. Name the state.

10. TRUE OR FALSE: The Twenty-sixth Amendment gave eighteen-year-olds the right to vote.

QUIZ 59

The Gettysburg Address

☆ ☆ ☆ ☆ ☆

Abraham Lincoln delivers the Gettysburg Address.

Answer the following questions about the speech the *Springfield Republican* described as "deep in feeling, compact in thought and expression, and tasteful and elegant in every word and comma." The Gettysburg Address is now universally considered to be one of the most profound and immortal expressions of humankind. (For reference, the complete Gettysburg Address is reprinted at the end of this quiz.)

1. What was the occasion for which Lincoln wrote and delivered the Gettysburg Address?

2. What was the date of the Gettysburg Address?

3. What one word did President Lincoln use five times in his Gettysburg Address?

4. How many manuscript copies of the Gettysburg Address are known to exist?

5. The Gettysburg Address has been officially translated into twenty-nine languages. Name as many of these languages as you can.

6. How long is "four score and seven years" and what significance did it have in Lincoln's address?

7. Lincoln made one statement in the Gettysburg Address which we now know to be blatantly false (although at the time he had no way of knowing this). What did he say?

8. TRUE OR FALSE: No known picture of Lincoln at Gettysburg exists.

9. TRUE OR FALSE: Abraham Lincoln was not the originator of the phrase "of the people, by the people, for the people."

10. Who invited President Lincoln to speak at Gettysburg?

The Gettysburg Address
by Abraham Lincoln

Four score and seven years ago our fathers brought forth, upon this continent, a new nation, conceived in Liberty and dedicated to the proposition that all men are created equal.

Now we are engaged in a great civil war, testing whether that nation, or any nation, so conceived, and so dedicated, can long endure. We are met here on a great battle-field of that war. We have come to dedicate a portion of it as a final resting place for those who here gave their lives that that nation might live. It is altogether fitting and proper that we should do this.

But in a larger sense we can not dedicate—we can not consecrate—we can not hallow this ground. The brave men, living and dead, who struggled here, have consecrated it far above our poor power to add or detract. The world will little note, nor long remember, what we say here, but can never forget what they did here. It is for us, the living, rather to be dedicated here to the unfinished work which they have, thus far, so nobly carried on. It is rather for us to be here dedicated to the great task remaining before us—that from these honored dead we take increased devotion to that cause for which they here gave the last full measure of devotion—that we here highly resolve that these dead shall not have died in vain; that this nation shall have a new birth of freedom; and that this government of the people, by the people, for the people shall not perish from the earth.

The Louisiana Purchase

THE
LOUISIANA
PURCHASE

A map of the Louisiana Purchase—France is still kicking herself for letting it go so cheaply.

1. What was the official date of the Louisiana Purchase?

   a. May 2, 1803   c. May 2, 1805

   b. May 2, 1804   d. May 2, 1806

2. What did the United States purchase in the Louisiana Purchase?

   a. The city of New Orleans

   b. A territory of the western United States extending from the Mississippi River to the Rocky Mountains between the Gulf of Mexico and the Canadian border

    c. The state of Florida, and all its ports

    d. Georgia, Alabama, and Arkansas

3. The two men who negotiated the Louisiana Purchase were James _____ and _____ Livingston.

4. Which U.S. President initiated the Louisiana Purchase?

    a. George Washington   c. Thomas Jefferson

    b. John Adams   d. James Madison

5. TRUE OR FALSE: The Louisiana Purchase was made because of fears that Napoleon intended to establish a North American empire.

6. What was the amount the United States paid in the Louisiana Purchase?

    a. $15 million cash

    b. $20 million cash

    c. $10 million cash, $5 million in gold

    d. $11,250,00 in cash and the assumption of $3,750,000 the French owed the American people

7. TRUE OR FALSE: The Louisiana Purchase only added a small area of land to the United States and was executed purely as a strategic move.

8. After the Louisiana Purchase, who was given the assignment of officially exploring the new U.S. territory?

9. Thirteen new states were carved out of the territory acquired in the Louisiana Purchase. Name them.

10. Where was the Louisiana Purchase cession Treaty signed?

    a. New Orleans   c. Boston

    b. Paris   d. London

The Monroe Doctrine

☆ ☆ ☆ ☆ ☆

1. TRUE OR FALSE: There is no American document known as the Monroe Doctrine.

2. What was the date that the Monroe Doctrine became known to the world?
   a. December 2, 1821
   b. December 2, 1822
   c. December 2, 1823
   d. December 2, 1824

3. State the Monroe Doctrine in ten words or less.

4. Who was responsible for drafting the majority of the message of the Monroe Doctrine?
   a. U.S. Secretary of State John Quincy Adams
   b. U.S. Secretary of War John Calhoun
   c. Vice President Daniel Tompkins
   d. Attorney General William Wirt

5. TRUE OR FALSE: In his Monroe Doctrine, President Monroe promised not to intervene in the affairs of established European colonies.

6. TRUE OR FALSE: One of the reasons President Monroe and his administration saw the necessity of proclaiming the Monroe Doctrine was because Russia had begun boldly moving into the northwest section of North America, into areas that the United States had previously claimed as being part of America.

7. Who said the following?

   "Any country whose people conduct themselves well, can count upon our hearty friendship. If a nation shows that it knows how to act with reasonable efficiency and decency in social and political manners, if it keeps order and pays its obligations, it need fear no interference from the United States. Chronic wrongdoing or an impotence which results in general loosening of the ties of civilized society, may in America, as elsewhere, ultimately require intervention by some civilized nation, and in the Western Hemisphere the adherence of the United States to the Monroe Doctrine may force the United States, however reluctantly, in flagrant cases of such wrongdoing or impotence, to exercise of an international power."

8. What was the term used to describe President Monroe's first term in office?

   a. The "America the Safe" Era

   b. The "Steamboat" Years

   c. The "America for America" Years

   d. The "Era of Good Feeling"

9. TRUE OR FALSE: According to political scientists and historians, in the decades following President Monroe's Monroe Doctrine, the Doctrine has been employed by the U.S. government to take over the management of the finances of the Dominican Republic and Nicaragua, and to occupy the republic of Haiti.

10. TRUE OR FALSE: The Monroe Doctrine was never accepted as valid international law by any European nation.

XI

The American Flag

QUIZ 62

The American Flag:
A Star-Spangled Quiz

☆ ☆ ☆ ☆ ☆

1. The American flag is one of the oldest flags in the world. Only three nation's flags are older. Name these three countries.

   a. Great Britain
   b. Sweden
   c. Denmark
   d. Spain
   e. The Netherlands

2. Congress first authorized the Flag of the United States on June 14th of what year?

   a. 1775
   b. 1776
   c. 1777
   d. 1778

3. What was the first official display of the new Flag of the United States?

   a. The Continental Army hoisted it over Fort Stanwix, New York on August 3, 1777.

   b. The Continental Congress raised it above the Philadelphia Capitol Building on July 4, 1776.

   c. George Washington raised it over the Continental Army's winter quarters at Valley Forge, Pennsylvania on December 17, 1777.

   d. The flag was raised in Philadelphia on November 15, 1777 after the Continental Congress endorsed the Articles of Confederation.

4. Who wrote the national anthem, "The Star-Spangled Banner"?

5. When was "The Star-Spangled Banner" officially made the U.S. national anthem?

6. How many stripes are on the U.S. flag and what are their colors?

7. What do the stripes on the flag symbolize?

8. TRUE OR FALSE: The first person to refer to the flag as Old Glory was a sea captain from Salem, Massachusetts named William Driver.

9. What is the proper way to dispose of a worn or damaged American flag?

10. TRUE OR FALSE: The United States can never exceed fifty states because there is no way of adding fifty-one stars to the flag.

QUIZ 73

Flag Protocol

☆ ☆ ☆ ☆ ☆

1. TRUE OR FALSE: When raising a flag to half-staff, it should be raised briskly to the halfway point of the staff and then secured.

2. When a flag is displayed with its union (the field of stars) downward, it means which of the following?
   a. It is a sign of mourning.
   b. It indicates the President of the United States is present.
   c. It is a distress signal.
   d. It indicates that Congress is in session.

3. How many guns are fired during the National Salute to the flag?
   a. Seven
   b. Twenty-one
   c. Fifty
   d. One

4. TRUE OR FALSE: When the President is not in Washington, D.C., the flag outside the White House does not fly.

5. On June 20, 1782, Charles Thomson, Secretary of the Continental Congress, stated in a report to Congress the meaning of the flag's colors. Match the color with its meaning:
   1. Red
   2. White
   3. Blue

   a. Purity and innocence
   b. Vigilance, perserverance, and justice
   c. Hardiness and valor

6. What do the flag's thirteen stripes represent?

    a. The first thirteen colonies of the United States

    b. The number of signers of the Declaration of Independence

    c. The number of days it took Betsy Ross to stitch the first flag

    d. The number of delegates to the first Constitutional Convention

7. TRUE OR FALSE: On Memorial Day, the flag should be displayed at half-staff until noon.

8. TRUE OR FALSE: A flag is never supposed to be displayed outside of polling places on election days.

9. What is the United States' official National March?

    a. "The Star-Spangled Banner"

    b. "America the Beautiful"

    c. "The Stars and Stripes Forever"

    d. "God Bless America"

10. An All-American Challenger: What is the name of the only person who has ever been honored for cutting an American flag into pieces?

XII

An All-American Potpourri

QUIZ 64

The Ten Greatest American Speeches Quiz

☆ ☆ ☆ ☆ ☆

As the end of the twentieth century neared, Texas A&M University and the University of Wisconsin–Madison conducted a survey of 137 rhetoric experts and asked them to name the most important and influential speeches of the twentieth century. Artistry was to be factored in as part of their selections. Your job is to identify the speaker of the speech from the clues provided in the following ten questions. **Note**: Forgive the seemingly shameless plug, but if you have a copy of my book, *The U.S.A. Book of Lists* (New Page Books), this quiz will be a lot easier to solve.

1. This 1963 speech was about racial equality and included the lines, "I have a dream that one day this nation will rise up and live out the true meaning of its creed. We hold these truths to be self-evident that all men are created equal."

2. This 1961 speech was an Inaugural Address and included the lines, "Ask not what your country can do for you; ask what you can do for your country."

3. This 1933 speech was an Inaugural Address and included the line, ". . . the only thing we have to fear is fear itself."

4. This 1941 speech was in response to an unprovoked attack and included the line, "Yesterday, December 7, 1941—a date which will live in infamy—the United States of America was suddenly and deliberately attacked by naval and air forces of the Empire of Japan."

5. This speech was the keynote address at the 1976 Democratic National Convention and included the passage, "I am going to close my speech by quoting a Republican President and I ask that as you listen to these words of Abraham Lincoln, relate them to the concept of national community in which every last one of us participates: 'As I would not not be a slave, so I would not be a master. This expresses my idea of Democracy. Whatever differs from this, to the extent of the difference is no Democracy.'"

6. This 1952 speech was delivered in response to accusations of financial irregularities and included the passage, "I owe $3,500 to my parents, and the interest on that loan, which I pay regularly, because it is a part of the savings they made through the years they were working so hard—I pay regularly 4 percent interest. And then I have a $500 loan, which I have on my life insurance. Well, that's about it. That's what we have. And that's what we owe. It isn't very much."

7. This 1964 speech was about civil rights and included the passage, "If we don't do something real soon, I think you'll have to agree that we're going to be forced either to use the ballot or the bullet. It's one or the other in 1964. It isn't that time is running out— time has run out! 1964 threatens to be the most explosive year America has ever witnessed."

8. This 1986 speech was in response to a national tragedy and included the passage, "For the families of the seven, we cannot bear, as you do, the full impact of this tragedy. But we feel the loss, and we're thinking about you so very much. Your loved ones were daring and brave, and they had that special grace, that special spirit that says, 'Give me a challenge and I'll meet it with joy.' They had a hunger to explore the universe and discover its truths. They wished to serve, and they did. They served all of us."

9. This 1960 speech was about religion and included the passage, "I believe in an America that is officially neither Catholic, Protestant nor Jewish—where no public official either requests or accepts instructions on public policy from the Pope, the National Council of Churches or any other ecclesiastical source—where no religious

body seeks to impose its will directly or indirectly upon the general populace or the public acts of its officials—and where religious liberty is so indivisible that an act against one church is treated as an act against all."

10. This 1965 speech was about voting rights and included the passage, "There is no constitutional issue here. The command of the Constitution is plain. There is no moral issue. It is wrong—deadly wrong—to deny any of your fellow Americans the right to vote in this country. There is no issue of States rights or national rights. There is only the struggle for human rights."

QUIZ 65

The First Ladies

☆ ☆ ☆ ☆ ☆

**Former First Lady
Eleanor Roosevelt**

Match the President with his First Lady . . . or, in a half dozen cases, First *Ladies*! (**Note:** There are only forty Presidents listed because Grover Cleveland was elected twice and James Buchanan never married.)

1. George Washington

    a. Abigail Smith

2. John Adams

    b. Lucy Ware Webb

3. Thomas Jefferson

    c. Lucretia Rudolph

4. James Madison

    d. Frances Folsom

5. James Monroe

    e. Hannah Hoes

6. John Quincy Adams

    f. Mary Scott Lord Dimmick

7. Andrew Jackson

    g. Florence Kling DeWolfe

8. Martin Van Buren

9. William Henry Harrison

10. John Tyler

11. James K. Polk

12. Zachary Taylor

13. Millard Fillmore

14. Franklin Pierce

15. Abraham Lincoln

16. Andrew Johnson

17. Ulysses S. Grant

18. Rutherford B. Hayes

19. James A. Garfield

20. Chester A. Arthur

21. Grover Cleveland

22. Benjamin Harrison

23. William McKinley

24. Theodore Roosevelt

25. William Howard Taft

26. Woodrow Wilson

27. Warren G. Harding

28. Calvin Coolidge

29. Herbert C. Hoover

30. Franklin D. Roosevelt

31. Harry S. Truman

32. Dwight D. Eisenhower

h. Lou Henry

i. Bess Wallace

j. Mamie Geneva Doud

k. Grace Anna Goodhue

l. Martha Dandridge Custis

m. Elizabeth "Eliza" Kortright

n. Dorothy "Dolley" Payne Todd

o. Margaret Smith

p. Anna Eleanor Roosevelt

q. Letitia Christian

r. Ellen Lewis Herndon

s. Rachel Donelson Robards

t. Julia Gardiner

u. Ida Saxton

v. Caroline Lavinia Scott

w. Alice Hathaway Lee

x. Helen Herron

y. Ellen Louise Axson

z. Jane Means Appleton

aa. Sarah Childress

bb. Mary Todd

cc. Martha Wayles Skelton

dd. Edith Bolling Galt

ee. Julia Dent

33. John F. Kennedy

34. Lyndon B. Johnson

35. Richard M. Nixon

36. Gerald R. Ford

37. James E. Carter, Jr.

38. Ronald W. Reagan

39. George H. W. Bush

40. William J. Clinton

ff. Anna Symmes

gg. Abigail Powers

hh. Edith Kermit Carow

ii. Caroline Carmichael McIntosh

jj. Jane Wyman

kk. Elizabeth "Betty" Bloomer Warren

ll. Claudia Alta "Lady Bird" Taylor

mm. Thelma Catherine "Pat" Ryan

nn. Louisa Catherine Johnson

oo. Jacqueline Lee Bouvier

pp. Eliza McCardle

qq. Rosalynn Smith

rr. Hillary Rodham

ss. Nancy Davis

tt. Barbara Pierce

The Presidents' Children

Identify the Presidential child from the information in each question.

1. This Presidential child was elected sixth President of the United States.

2. This Presidential child was married in the first wedding ever performed in the White House.

3. This Presidential child was the only man ever to be the son of a President and the father of a President.

4. This Presidential child was the Assistant Secretary of War *for the Confederacy* during the Civil War.

5. This Presidential child was War Secretary from 1881 to 1885.

6. This Presidential child authored the 1925 book, *In the Days of My Father General Grant.*

7. This Presidential child was given the nickname "Baby Ruth" by the press shortly after her birth.

8. This Presidential child was Assistant Secretary of the Navy from 1921 to 1925.

9. This Presidential child was arrested for being involved in illegal protests as a student at Brown University.

10. These Presidential children are twin girls and the granddaughters of a former President.

QUIZ 67

American National Parks

☆ ☆ ☆ ☆ ☆

How long do you think it would take to visit every American National Park if you visited one a month, every month? If you started in January 2004, you would visit your last park in September 2038. It would take 34 years and 9 months to visit all 417 National Parks at the rate of one a month. (It would only take you eight years to visit every park if you somehow were able to manage the superhuman pace of visiting one park each week.)

Match one of the 128 U.S. National Parks from the left column with the state where it is located in the right column. (**Note:** Some states have multiple parks on the list.)

1. Abraham Lincoln Birthplace National Historic Site

2. Agate Fossil Beds National Monument

3. Alcatraz Island

4. Aleutian World War II

5. Amistad National Recreation Area

6. Andrew Johnson National Historic Site

7. Antietam National Cemetery

8. Aztec Ruins National Monument

a. Alaska

b. Alabama

c. Arkansas

d. Arizona

e. California

f. Colorado

g. Connecticut

h. Washington, D.C.

i. Florida

j. Georgia

k. Hawaii

9. Badlands National Park

10. Big Hole National Battlefield

11. Booker T. Washington National Monument

12. Canaveral National Seashore

13. Cane River Creole National Historical Park

14. Carl Sandburg Home National Historic Site

15. Carlsbad Caverns National Park

16. Charles Pinckney National Historic Site

17. Chickamauga and Chattanooga National Military Park

18. City of Rocks National Reserve

19. Clara Barton National Historic Site

20. Constitution Gardens

21. Crater Lake National Park

22. Craters of The Moon National Monument

23. Cumberland Gap National Historical Park

24. Dayton Aviation Heritage National Historical Park

25. Death Valley National Park

l. Iowa

m. Idaho

n. Illinois

o. Indiana

p. Kansas

q. Kentucky

r. Louisiana

s. Massachusetts

t. Maryland

u. Maine

v. Michigan

w. Minnesota

x. Missouri

y. Mississippi

z. Montana

aa. North Carolina

bb. North Dakota

cc. Nebraska

dd. New Jersey

ee. New Mexico

ff. Nevada

gg. New York

hh. Ohio

ii. Oklahoma

jj. Oregon

26. Dinosaur National Monument

27. Edgar Allan Poe National Historic Site

28. Edison National Historic Site

29. Effigy Mounds National Monument

30. Eisenhower National Historic Site

31. Eleanor Roosevelt National Historic Site

32. Ellis Island National Monument

33. Eugene O'Neill National Historic Site

34. Everglades National Park

35. Fire Island National Seashore

36. First Ladies National Historic Site

37. Ford's Theatre National Historic Site

38. Fort Smith National Historic Site

39. Franklin Delano Roosevelt Memorial

40. Frederick Douglass National Historic Site

41. Frederick Law Olmsted National Historic Site

kk. Pennsylvania

ll. Rhode Island

mm. South Carolina

nn. South Dakota

oo. Tennessee

pp. Texas

qq. Utah

rr. Virginia

42. General Grant National Memorial

43. George Washington Birthplace National Monument

44. George Washington Carver National Monument

45. Gettysburg National Cemetery

46. Glacier Bay National Park and Preserve

47. Glacier National Park

48. Golden Gate National Recreation Area

49. Golden Spike National Historic Site

50. Grand Canyon National Park

51. Great Basin National Park

52. Great Smoky Mountains National Park

53. Guadalupe Mountains National Park

54. Harry S. Truman National Historic Site

55. Herbert Hoover National Historic Site

56. Home of Franklin D. Roosevelt National Historic Site

57. Hot Springs National Park

58. James A. Garfield National Historic Site

59. Jean Lafitte National Historic Park and Preserve

60. Jefferson National Expansion Memorial

61. Jimmy Carter National Historic Site

62. John F. Kennedy National Historic Site

63. Johnstown Flood National Memorial

64. Joshua Tree National Park

65. Klondike Gold Rush National Historical Park

66. Korean War Veterans Memorial

67. Lava Beds National Monument

68. Lewis & Clark National Historic Trail

69. Lincoln Boyhood National Memorial

70. Lincoln Home National Historic Site

71. Lincoln Memorial

72. Little Bighorn Battlefield National Monument

73. Longfellow National Historic Site

74. Lowell National Historical Park

75. Lyndon B. Johnson National Historical Park

76. Lyndon Baines Johnson Memorial Grove on the Potomac

77. Martin Luther King, Jr. National Historic Site

78. Martin Van Buren National Historic Site

79. Mesa Verde National Park

80. Minute Man National Historical Park

81. Minuteman Missile National Historic Site

82. Montezuma Castle National Monument

83. Mormon Pioneer National Historic Trail

84. Mount Rushmore National Memorial

85. National Historic Area

86. National Mall

87. Natural Bridges National Monument

88. Navajo National Monument

89. Nicodemus National Historic Site

90. Organ Pipe Cactus National Monument

91. Ozark National Scenic Riverways

92. Pecos National Historical Park

93. Petrified Forest National Park

94. Pictured Rocks National Lakeshore

95. Pipestone National Monument

96. Pony Express National Historic Trail

97. Pu`uhonua O Honaunau National Historical Park

98. Quinebaug & Shetucket Rivers Valley National Heritage Corridor

99. Rainbow Bridge National Monument

100. Rocky Mountain National Park

101. Roger Williams National Memorial

102. Roosevelt Campobello International Park

103. Rosie the Riveter WWII Home Front National Historical Park

104. Selma to Montgomery National Historic Trail

105. Shiloh National Cemetery

106. Sleeping Bear Dunes National Lakeshore

107. Statue of Liberty National Monument

108. Tallgrass Prairie National Preserve

109. The Old Stone House

110. Theodore Roosevelt Birthplace National Historic Site

111. Theodore Roosevelt Island Park

112. Theodore Roosevelt National Park

113. Thomas Jefferson Memorial

114. Thomas Stone National Historic Site

115. Trail of Tears National Historic Trail

116. Tupelo National Battlefield

117. Tuskegee Airmen National Historic Site

118. USS *Arizona* Memorial

119. Ulysses S. Grant National Historic Site

120. Vicksburg National Cemetery

121. Vietnam Veterans Memorial

122. Washington Monument

123. Washita Battlefield National Historic Site

124. White Sands National Monument

125. William Howard Taft National Historic Site

126. Women's Rights National Historical Park

127. Wright Brothers National Memorial

128. Yosemite National Park

Which American Said It?

☆ ☆ ☆ ☆ ☆

Match the quotation from the left with the American from the right who said it.

1. "If I could save the Union without freeing *any* slave, I would do it; and if I could save it by freeing *all* the slaves, I would do it; and if I could do it by freeing some and leaving others alone, I would do that. . . . I have here stated my purpose according to my *official* duty, and I intend no modification of my oft-expressed *personal* wish that all men, everywhere, could be free."

2. "The art of making love, muffled up in furs, in the open air, with the thermometer at Zero, is a Yankee invention, which requires a Yankee poet to describe."

3. "I have a dream that one day this nation will rise up and live out the true meaning of its creed: 'We hold these truths to be self-evident: that all men are created equal.'"

4. "I was affected with Montezuma's revenge."

a. John Quincy Adams

b. Jimmy Carter

c. Casey Stengel

d. Adlai Stevenson

e. B. F. Skinner

f. Phyllis Schafly

g. Calvin Klein

h. Kurt Vonnegut

i. Thomas Jefferson

j. Abraham Lincoln

k. Frank Lloyd Wright

l. Martin Luther King, Jr.

m. Tennessee Williams

n. Lillian Hellman

o. Ronald Reagan

p. Thomas Edison

5. "I think [the women's movement is] an antifamily movement that is trying to make perversion acceptable as an alternate life-style."

6. "War is fear cloaked in courage."

7. "I guess this means they fired me. I'll never make the mistake of being seventy years old again."

8. "Nature is neutral. Man has wrested from nature the power to make the world a desert or to make the deserts bloom. There is no evil in the atom; only in men's souls."

9. "You can be young without money but you can't be old without it."

10. "I think there's something incredibly sexy about a woman wearing her boyfriend's t-shirt and underwear."

11. "A great many people in Los Angeles are on strict diets that restrict their intake of synthetic foods. The reason for this appears to be a widely held belief that organically grown fruit and vegetables make the cocaine work faster."

12. "Of all the cankers of human happiness, none corrodes it with so silent, yet so baneful a tooth, as indolence. . . . Idleness begets ennui, ennui the hypochondria, and that a diseased body."

q. Gloria Steinem

r. Ernest Hemingway

s. General William C. Westmoreland

t. Fran Lebowitz

u. Pearl S. Buck

v. Joseph Heller

w. Harry S. Truman

x. James Thurber

y. John F. Kennedy

13. "I did not want to read about the war.
    I was going to forget the war.
    I had made a separate peace."

14. "The physician can bury his mistakes,
    but the architect can only advise his
    clients to plant vines."

15. "The definition of woman's work is
    shitwork."

16. "Fashions in sin change."

17. "What kind of peace do we seek? Not
    a *Pax Americana* enforced on the
    world by American weapons of war.
    Not the peace of the grave or the
    security of the slave. I am talking
    about genuine peace, the kind of
    peace that makes life on earth worth
    living, the kind that enable men and
    nations to grow and to hope to build a
    better life for their children—not
    merely peace in our time, but peace
    for all time."

18. "I never did anything worth doing
    by accident, nor did any of my
    inventions come by accident; they
    came by work."

19. "Well all the President is, is a glorified
    public relations man who spends his
    time flattering, kissing, and kicking
    people to get them to do what they
    are supposed to do anyway."

20. "Discussion in America means
    dissent."

21. "Effeminacy is not a feminine possession any more than a masculine one. Men or women become effeminate when privilege and lack of responsibility have made them weak. The true female creature, unspoiled, is tough, persistent, and strong."

22. "People don't start wars, governments do."

23. "The real problem is not whether machines think but whether men do."

24. "Good God, how much reverence can you have for a Supreme Being who finds it necessary to include such phenomena as phlegm and tooth decay in his divine system of Creation?"

25. "'One sacred thing from childhood is perhaps the best education,' said Fyodor Dostoevsky. I believe that, and I hope that many Earthling children will respond to the first human footprint on the moon as a sacred thing. We need sacred things."

American National Monuments

☆ ☆ ☆ ☆ ☆

"Can someone get this fly off my nose?"
Mount Rushmore, an American monument.

1. Which of the following U.S. Presidents is *not* on Mount Rushmore?
   a. Abraham Lincoln
   b. Ulysses S. Grant
   c. George Washington
   d. Theodore Roosevelt
   e. Thomas Jefferson

2. TRUE OR FALSE: In honor of its large Korean population, the Korean War Veterans Memorial is located in Dulles, Texas.

3. The Lincoln Memorial has thirty-six marble Doric columns. What does the number thirty-six represent?

   a. The number of states in the Union at the time of Lincoln's death

   b. The number of paragraphs in Lincoln's Gettysburg Address

   c. The number of steps of the Capitol Building

   d. The number of Union battle victories during the Civil War

4. Which two of these documents are inscribed on the Lincoln Memorial?

   a. Lincoln's First Inaugural Address

   b. The Gettysburg Address

   c. The Emancipation Proclamation

   d. Lincoln's Second Inaugural Address

5. TRUE OR FALSE: The Vietnam Veterans Memorial was built using federal funds, appropriated by Congress in honor of those who lost their lives in Vietnam.

6. The cornerstone of the Washington Monument was laid in 1848, yet the construction of the obelisk was not completed until 1885. Why the delay?

   a. Lack of funds

   b. Disagreement over the Monument's height

   c. Public resistance to having a "neo-Egyptian"-style memorial in Washington

   d. The Civil War

7. TRUE OR FALSE: Before the USS *Arizona* Memorial at Pearl Harbor was built, the bodies of all the killed crewmen were removed from the sunken ship and buried at Arlington National Cemetery.

8. Which of the following is *not* an official U.S. National Memorial?

   a. Alcatraz Island

   b. The Rosie the Riveter WWII Home Front National Historical Park

   c. The Ford's Theatre National Historic Site

   d. The Jimmy Carter National Historical Site

   e. The Craters of the Moon National Memorial

   f. The Edgar Allan Poe National Historical Site

   g. None of the above. They are *all* National Memorials.

9. TRUE OR FALSE: The Statue of Liberty was a gift to the people of the United States from Francisco Franco.

10. Name the only U.S. National Monument established in honor of American dinosaurs.

   a. Jurassic Park in California

   b. Raptor National Park in Oregon

   c. Dinosaur National Monument in Colorado

   d. Mesozoic National Monument in New Mexico

QUIZ 70

American Food

☆ ☆ ☆ ☆ ☆

Identify the American food from the question or clue.

1. Peanuts and candied popcorn in a box.

2. This was the Campbell Soup Company's first soup.

3. This was the first caffeine-free coffee.

4. "RC Cola and a _____ _____."

5. This hamburger chain, which predated McDonald's by two decades, is famous for its square burgers.

6. "Ho, ho, ho, _____ _____!"

7. This tasty non-cola beverage was originally called Lithiated Lemon.

8. "Bet you can't eat just one."

9. "_____ are for kids!"

10. The astronaut's beverage.

11. "Two all-beef patties, special sauce, lettuce, cheese, pickles, onions on a sesame seed bun."

12. "Leggo my _____."

13. This candy was made a movie star and saw a huge increase in sales thanks to its appearance in *ET: The Extra-Terrestrial*. (Hint: M & Ms passed.)

14. Pork in a can; unwanted E-mail.

15. "Plop, plop, fizz, fizz, oh, what a relief it is."

QUIZ 71

American Tourist Attractions

☆ ☆ ☆ ☆ ☆

Match the following thirty-one weird American tourist attractions from the left column with their location in this great land of ours from the right column. (Every one of these places is a real, honest-to-Jehosaphat place that you can actually visit. Whether or not you want to is up to you, of course. **Hint:** This one is easier than it looks. Think outside . . . er, *inside* the box!)

1. The Atomic Bomb Crater

2. The Dan Blocker Memorial Head

3. The Donner Party Museum

4. The Five-Story-Tall Chicken

5. Flintstone Bedrock City

6. Frederick's Bra Museum

7. The Hair Museum

8. The Hall of Mosses

9. Hobbiton, U.S.A.

10. The Hoegh Pet Casket Company

11. Holy Land, U.S.A.

12. The House of Telephones

13. Jimi Hendrix Viewpoint

a. Mars Bluff, South Carolina

b. O'Donnell, Texas

c. Truckee, California

d. Marietta, Georgia

e. Vail, Arizona

f. Hollywood, California

g. Independence, Missouri

h. Port Angeles, Washington

i. Phillipsville, California

j. Gladstone, Michigan

k. Waterbury, Connecticut

l. Coffeyville, Kansas

m. Seattle, Washington

n. Las Vegas, Nevada

14. The Liberace Museum

15. The Museum of Questionable Medical Devices

16. The Nut Museum

17. Philip Morris Cigarette Tours

18. The Soup Tureen Museum

19. The Spam Museum

20. Spongeorama

21. The Testicle Festival

22. Toilet Rock

23. The Tupperware Awareness Center

24. The Urinal Used by JFK

25. The Wonderful World of Tiny Horses

26. The World's Largest Artichoke

27. The World's Largest Chest of Drawers

28. The World's Largest Crucifix

29. The World's Largest Office Chair

30. The World's Largest Stump

31. The World's Largest Twine Ball

o. Minneapolis, Minnesota

p. Old Lyme, Connecticut

q. Richmond, Virginia

r. Camden, New Jersey

s. Austin, Minnesota

t. Tarpon Springs, Florida

u. Clinton, Montana

v. City of Rocks, New Mexico

w. Kissimmee, Florida

x. Salem, Ohio

y. Eureka Springs, Arkansas

z. Castroville, California

aa. High Point, North Carolina

bb. Bardstown, Kentucky

cc. Anniston, Alabama

dd. Kokomo, Indiana

ee. Darwin, Minnesota

QUIZ 72

American Geography

☆ ☆ ☆ ☆ ☆

1. What are the "four corners" states?

2. Name the two states that flank Lake Michigan on its east and west sides.

3. Rhode Island is the smallest U.S. state. What is the *second* smallest state?

4. Alaska is the largest U.S. state. What is the *second* largest state?

5. What geographical feature do the following ten states all have in common?

   Hawaii, Oregon, Texas, Georgia, Virginia, New Jersey, Indiana, Maine, Pennsylvania, and Minnesota.

6. TRUE OR FALSE: As of July 1999, the U.S. state with the lowest population was Wyoming.

7. TRUE OR FALSE: The state of Idaho borders Canada.

8. Is Florida in the Eastern or Central Time Zone?

9. From this list of twenty-six states, identify the thirteen original states:

   1. Alabama
   2. California
   3. Colorado
   4. Connecticut
   5. Delaware
   6. Florida
   7. Georgia
   8. Illinois
   9. Kansas
   10. Louisiana
   11. Maine
   12. Maryland
   13. Massachusetts
   14. Nevada
   15. New Hampshire
   16. New Jersey
   17. New Mexico
   18. New York
   19. North Carolina
   20. North Dakota
   21. Oregon
   22. Pennsylvania
   23. Rhode Island
   24. South Carolina
   25. Texas
   26. Virginia

10. What state was known as "Seward's Folly"?

QUIZ 73

State Motto Quiz

☆ ☆ ☆ ☆ ☆

Match the U.S. state from the left column with its motto from the right column.

1. Alabama

2. Alaska

3. Arizona

4. Arkansas

5. California

6. Colorado

7. Connecticut

8. Delaware

9. District of Columbia

10. Florida

11. Georgia

12. Hawaii

13. Idaho

14. Illinois

15. Indiana

16. Iowa

17. Kansas

a. North to the Future

b. The Life of the Land Is Perpetuated by Righteousness

c. Our Liberties We Prize and Our Rights We Will Maintain

d. The Star of the North

e. State Sovereignty—National Union

f. I Direct

g. Liberty and Independence

h. Ever Upward

i. Equality Before the Law

j. We Dare to Defend Our Rights

k. Thus Always to Tyrants

l. God Enriches

m. Nothing Without Providence

18. Kentucky

19. Louisiana

20. Maine

21. Maryland

22. Massachusetts

23. Michigan

24. Minnesota

25. Mississippi

26. Missouri

27. Montana

28. Nebraska

29. Nevada

30. New Hampshire

31. New Jersey

32. New Mexico

33. New York

34. North Carolina

35. North Dakota

36. Ohio

37. Oklahoma

38. Oregon

39. Pennsylvania

40. Rhode Island

41. South Carolina

42. South Dakota

n. With God, All Things Are Possible

o. The Union

p. Eureka . . . I Have Found It

q. Prepared In Mind and Resources

r. United We Stand, Divided We Fall

s. By the Sword We Seek Peace, but Peace Only under Liberty

t. The Welfare of the People Shall Be the Supreme Law

u. Liberty and Prosperity

v. Let the People Rule

w. Live Free or Die

x. It Grows as It Goes

y. May She Endure Forever

z. The Crossroads of America

aa. If You Seek a Pleasant Peninsula, Look around You

bb. To Be, Rather Than to Seem

cc. Justice to All

dd. Gold and Silver

ee. Friendship

ff. In God We Trust

43. Tennessee

44. Texas

45. Utah

46. Vermont

47. Virginia

48. Washington

49. West Virginia

50. Wisconsin

51. Wyoming

gg. Forward

hh. He Who Transplanted Sustains

ii. Manly Deeds, Womanly Words

jj. Liberty and Union, Now and Forever, One and Inseparable

kk. All for Our Country

ll. Hope

mm. America at Its Best

nn. Industry

oo. Freedom and Unity

pp. Bye and Bye

qq. To the Stars Through Difficulties

rr. Mountaineers Are Always Free

ss. Union, Justice, and Confidence

tt. Under God the People Rule

uu. Virtue, Liberty, and Independence

vv. Work Conquers All Things

ww. Wisdom, Justice, and Moderation

xx. By Valor and Arms

yy. Equal Rights

The State Capitals Quiz

✰ ✰ ✰ ✰ ✰

Match the state from the left column with its capital city from the right column.

1. Alabama	a.	Albany
2. Alaska	b.	Annapolis
3. Arizona	c.	Atlanta
4. Arkansas	d.	Augusta
5. California	e.	Austin
6. Colorado	f.	Baton Rouge
7. Connecticut	g.	Bismarck
8. Delaware	h.	Boise
9. Florida	i.	Boston
10. Georgia	j.	Carson City
11. Hawaii	k.	Charleston
12. Idaho	l.	Cheyenne
13. Illinois	m.	Columbia
14. Indiana	n.	Columbus
15. Iowa	o.	Concord
16. Kansas	p.	Denver
17. Kentucky	q.	Des Moines

18.	Louisiana	r.	Dover
19.	Maine	s.	Frankfort
20.	Maryland	t.	Harrisburg
21.	Massachusetts	u.	Hartford
22.	Michigan	v.	Helena
23.	Minnesota	w.	Honolulu
24.	Mississippi	x.	Indianapolis
25.	Missouri	y.	Jackson
26.	Montana	z.	Jefferson City
27.	Nebraska	aa.	Juneau
28.	Nevada	bb.	Lansing
29.	New Hampshire	cc.	Lincoln
30.	New Jersey	dd.	Little Rock
31.	New Mexico	ee.	Madison
32.	New York	ff.	Montgomery
33.	North Carolina	gg.	Montpelier
34.	North Dakota	hh.	Nashville
35.	Ohio	ii.	Oklahoma City
36.	Oklahoma	jj.	Olympia
37.	Oregon	kk.	Phoenix
38.	Pennsylvania	ll.	Pierre
39.	Rhode Island	mm.	Providence
40.	South Carolina	nn.	Raleigh
41.	South Dakota	oo.	Richmond
42.	Tennessee	pp.	Sacramento

43. Texas	qq.	Salem
44. Utah	rr.	Salt Lake City
45. Vermont	ss.	Santa Fe
46. Virginia	tt.	Springfield
47. Washington	uu.	St. Paul
48. West Virginia	vv.	Tallahassee
49. Wisconsin	ww.	Topeka
50. Wyoming	xx.	Trenton

QUIZ 75

American Fads and Crazes

1. This exaggeratedly expressive dance, which had been originated by slaves as a way of making fun of their white masters' mannered and pompous ballroom dancing, was very popular in America in the late 1890s and early 1900s.

2. This incredibly popular turn-of-the-century toy rifle (the first toy gun ever made in metal) coined a catch phrase ("Clarence, it's a daisy!") and was eventually banned in all fifty states.

3. Which of the following legendary toys were first introduced in the first decade of the twentieth century?
   a. Lincoln Logs
   b. Tinkertoys
   c. Erector Set
   d. All of the above

4. This Spanish dance, popularized in the 1910s by Vern and Irene Castle, was banned in Boston because of its erotic innuendo.

5. This 1939 film adaptation of an international best-seller starred Clark Gable and Vivien Leigh.

6. In the mid-1940s, this female icon became the symbol for all the working women keeping the factories at home humming during wartime.

7. This hip-twirling plastic toy of the 1950s has been dubbed the "biggest fad in history."

8. Chubby Checker, who inspired this dance craze, once described it as follows: "It's like putting out a cigarette with both of your feet, and coming out of a shower and wiping your bottom with a towel to the beat of the music."

9. 1. Remove all your clothes. *All* of them. 2. Run down a city street, onto a football field, or across the stage at the Oscars. 3. Identify this craze.

10. These four reptile superheroes were each named for a great Renaissance painter.

The Library of Congress

☆ ☆ ☆ ☆ ☆

Read any good books lately? The Library of Congress.

1. After the original Congressional Library (later renamed the Library of Congress) was burned by the British in 1814, 6,487 books were purchased from a man who once proclaimed, "I cannot live without books." These books formed the basis of the new Library of Congress. Who was this man?

   a. Benjamin Franklin   c. John Adams

   b. Thomas Jefferson   d. James Madison

2. How much did the United States government pay for the 6,487 books for the new Library of Congress?

   a. $1   c. $100,000

   b. $23,950   d. Nothing. They were all donated.

3. TRUE OR FALSE: Access to the Library of Congress is restricted to American citizens.

4. TRUE OR FALSE: The Library of Congress is the largest library in the world.

5. How many items are in the Library of Congress?

   a. 5 million   c. 100 million

   b. 50 million   d. 126 million

6. How many items a day are added to the Library of Congress's collections?

   a. one thousand   c. eight thousand

   b. five thousand   d. ten thousand

7. The Library of Congress has the world's largest collection of a single type of musical instrument. What is this instrument?

   a. Violin   c. Drum

   b. Flute   d. Harpsichord

8. TRUE OR FALSE: The Library of Congress owns one of only three perfect copies of the Gutenberg Bible.

9. TRUE OR FALSE: The Library of Congress owns a book the size of the period at the end of this sentence.

10. BRAINBUSTER: Who is the current Librarian of Congress?

QUIZ 77

Famous American Women

Identify the famous American woman from the clue.

1. Lost aviator.

2. Nurse who founded the Red Cross.

3. Writer of *The Women* and U.S. Ambassador to Italy 1953–1956.

4. Mrs. FDR.

5. First American saint.

6. Abolitionist; led more than three hundred slaves to freedom via the Underground Railroad.

7. Senator and author of *Living History*.

8. Mrs. JFK.

9. Refused to sit at the back of the bus.

10. Nineteenth-century feminist and suffragette; now a dollar.

The Top Ten American Religions

☆ ☆ ☆ ☆ ☆

This quiz asks you to match the religious denomination from the left column with the number of its American adherents from the right column. (The numbers for this quiz were drawn from *The 1999 Yearbook of American & Canadian Churches*, published by the National Councils of Churches of Christ in the U.S.A.; and *The World Almanac and Book of Facts*, 2000 edition.)

1.	Baptist	a.	4,075,000
2.	Eastern Orthodox	b.	4,145,932
3.	Islam	c.	5,058,998
4.	Jewish	d.	5,171,623
5.	Latter-day Saints	e.	5,500,000
6.	Lutheran	f.	8,312,036
7.	Methodist	g.	10,396,628
8.	Pentecostal	h.	13,463,552
9.	Presbyterian	i.	33,064,341
10.	Roman Catholic	j.	61,207,914

American Superstitions

☆ ☆ ☆ ☆ ☆

How superstitious are you? Oh, you're not? You'll walk under a ladder with careless abandon? If you break a mirror you simply go out and buy a new one? You have never knocked wood?

The following questions are about American beliefs, superstitions, lore, and traditions.

As ridiculous as many of these sound, they are an enduring part of American culture and are still held to be true by many of our fellow citizens. (The superstitions covered in this quiz are drawn from information in a fascinating book called *Lightning Never Strikes Twice (If You Own a Feather Bed)* by Vergilius Ferm (Gramercy,1989).

1. According to a North Carolina superstition, what will happen if a woman bakes a cake when she is menstruating?
   a. Her oven will not work.
   b. The cake will not turn out right.
   c. Her kitchen will be overrun with spiders.
   d. She will forever lose her taste for all things sweet.

2. According to an Ohio superstition, what will cure chills and fever?
   a. A poultice of cow dung and red wine
   b. A slice of rye bread dunked in honey and sprinkled with red pepper
   c. A drink made of coffee and the seeds of a kumquat
   d. A mixture of bed bugs and beans

3. According to a western Pennsylvania superstition, bees target red-haired people and overlook what types of people?

   a. Fat people

   b. People with good dispositions

   c. Idiots

   d. Women with six toes

4. According to a Native American superstition, what does the sighting of an owl signify?

   a. A tornado

   c. Approaching death

   b. A crop failure

   d. A drought

5. According to a Pennsylvania superstition, what is the best day to plant cabbages to assure a successful crop?

   a. March 17th, St. Patrick's Day

   b. March 15th, the Ides of March

   c. The day after the first full moon in February

   d. The day before the first full moon in March

6. According to a Maine superstition, what is one of the best ways to cure a cold?

   a. Tie a dead fish skin to your feet.

   b. Place a black olive on each of your toes for two hours.

   c. Tie a scarf made from corn husks around your neck.

   d. Dunk your hand in blackstrap molasses and let the molasses drip onto a quahog shell.

7. According to a New England superstition, what is the best way to get a stuck fish bone out of your throat?

   a. Pull both your earlobes.

   b. Tap your right ankle with a clam shucker.

   c. Pull your left thumb.

   d. Pull your big toe.

8. According to a western U.S.A. superstition, what is the best day to plant potatoes to assure a successful crop?

   a. Ash Wednesday   c. Easter Sunday

   b. Good Friday   d. Easter Monday

9. According to North Carolina lore, what is a good way to prevent tears when peeling onions?

   a. Hold a piece of raw potato in your mouth.

   b. Hold a match between your teeth.

   c. Turn on the faucet and let the water run.

   d. All of the above

10. According to a Lousiana superstition, what are two of the best ways to rid a house of ants?

    a. Spit out the kitchen window three times while silently saying the Lord's Prayer.

    b. Throw coffee grounds under the steps to the kitchen.

    c. Put a pine cone in a cabinet closest to the kitchen door.

    d. Bring some ants in a leaf to a neighbor's house.

QUIZ 80

Famous African-Americans

Martin Luther King

1. Hit 755 home runs in his major league career.

2. Wrote a poem for Clinton's inauguration.

3. Satchmo.

4. American botanist, agricultural chemist, and educator who developed hundreds of uses for the peanut and other crops.

5. Won an Academy Award for her performance in *Monster's Ball*.

6. *Roots* author.

7. Civil rights leader; his birthday is a legal holiday celebrated in January.

8. George W. Bush's National Security Advisor.

9. American abolitionist and feminist. Born into slavery, she was freed in 1827 and became a leading preacher against slavery and for the rights of women.

10. Black Man in Black.

11. Some consider him the greatest golfer of all time.

12. American writer, poet, and playwright whose work, including *Weary Blues* (1926) and *The Ways of White Folks* (1934), made an important contribution to the Harlem Renaissance.

13. Talk show host, book club founder, and magazine publisher.

14. Educator of the late nineteenth and early twentieth centuries; founder of Tuskegee Institute; the best known of his many books is *Up from Slavery*.

15. Perhaps the greatest ragtime composer of all time.

American Disasters

1. TRUE OR FALSE: It has been conclusively confirmed that the Great Chicago Fire started in Mrs. Patrick O'Leary's barn on DeKoven Street on the West Side of Chicago around 9:00 P.M. on Sunday, October 8, 1871 when Mrs. O'Leary's cow kicked over an oil-filled lantern.

2. What were the three meteorological factors that made the 1888 Atlantic Seaboard blizzard a "once-in-five-hundred-years storm"?

3. What was the cause of the catastrophic 1889 Johnstown floods?

4. What magnitude was the 1906 San Francisco earthquake?

   a. 5.8   c. 7.5

   b. 8.3   d. 9.1

5. What was the amount of the damages awarded to the families of the 145 victims of the 1911 New York Triangle Shirtwaist Factory fire?

   a. $75   c. $50,000

   b. $5,000   d. $1,000,000

6. How did the Boston Cocoanut Grove nighclub fire start?

   a. The club was fire-bombed by a disgruntled employee.

   b. A sixteen-year-old busboy lit a match to change a lightbulb.

   c. A candle tipped over and ignited the crinoline lining of a woman's dress.

   d. An overloaded electrical outlet started sparking.

7. TRUE OR FALSE: The 1944 Ringling Brothers and Barnum and Bailey Circus fire was started by an arsonist named Robert Segee who was sentenced to forty-four years in prison.

8. TRUE OR FALSE: The 1947 Texas City Harbor explosion was so powerful it set off an earthquake seismic detector in Denver, Colorado, a thousand miles away.

9. Who was responsible for the 1995 Oklahoma City Murrah Federal Building bombing?

10. What happened on September 11, 2001?

QUIZ 82

Weird America

☆ ☆ ☆ ☆ ☆

1. According to believers, what happened in Roswell, New Mexico in July 1947?
   a. An alien spaceship crashed in the desert and the U.S. government recovered the ship and the bodies of aliens from the crash site.
   b. A UFO landed, kidnapped a group of hikers, and then took off.
   c. A time portal opened up and hikers were transported to Atlantis.
   d. Extraterrestrials executed a mass cattle mutilation.

2. What was the name of the pilot who saw nine objects flying in formation over Washington state in 1947, ushering in the modern UFO age?

3. Where is Area 51?
   a. Seattle, Washington   c. Groom Lake, Nevada
   b. Sacramento, California   d. Tucson, Arizona

4. TRUE OR FALSE: President Jimmy Carter once saw a UFO and filed an official report.

5. TRUE OR FALSE: The United States government is not currently officially investigating UFO sightings.

6. The ghost of which U.S. President has been seen in the White House more times than any other?

a. George Washington   c. Abraham Lincoln

b. Ulysses S. Grant   d. John F. Kennedy

7. What is the large, hairy, humanlike creature purported to inhabit the Pacific Northwest called?

   a. Bigfoot   c. Yeti

   b. Sasquatch   d. All of the above

8. What was the name of the American researcher and writer who specialized in bizarre phenomena like ghosts, stigmata, rains of meat, levitation, teleportation and other oddities, and whose body of work is now known as "Forteana?"

9. Which of the following Abraham Lincoln/John F. Kennedy coincidences are true?

   a. Each President experienced the death of a son while president.

   b. Both Presidents were related to ambassadors to the Court of St. James in Great Britain.

   c. Both Presidents were buried in mahogany caskets.

   d. The assassins of the Presidents were each killed by a single shot from a Colt revolver.

   e. Both Presidents had been skippers of a boat.

   f. Both Presidents married socially prominent, twenty-four-year-old brunettes who were fluent in French, known for their fashion sense, and both of whom had been previously engaged.

   g. All of the above

10. TRUE OR FALSE: Completely nude photographs were taken of all incoming freshmen at Ivy League and Seven Sisters colleges from 1940 through 1960, including then-college students Hillary Rodham Clinton, Diane Sawyer, George Bush, and thousands of others, and these pictures still exist to this day.

Native American Contributions to American Culture

1. These *two* tubers are one of America's most popular vegetables. They are most commonly eaten baked, fried, or mashed.

2. This vegetable is not a vegetable, but actually a fruit. Italians use a lot of these.

3. This bitter drug is used to treat malaria and is also used to treat night leg cramps.

4. This type of Native American shelter was adopted by the U.S military for bivouacking.

5. This swinging "bed" allows you to take a nap between two trees.

6. This popular snow travel vehicle is a runnerless sled with two boards curved up in the front.

7. Need to vomit? Grab a bottle of this!

8. This bean now gives us the most popular ice cream flavor.

9. This soft leather footwear might be one of the most comfortable shoes of all time.

10. This blanket-like cloak is now commonly used as rainwear.

The Ultimate Red, White & Blue IQ Test

This quiz is a potpourri, a hodgepodge, a farrago, a conglomeration—a mixed bag of eighty miscellaneous questions about America and her people, places, things, and events.

1. What Supreme Court case ultimately resulted in the publication of the *Pentagon Papers*?
   a. *Korematsu v. United States*
   b. The Alien Registration Act
   c. *Schenck v. United States*
   d. *New York Times v. United States*

2. Who was the first black woman elected to Congress?
   a. Harriet Tubman
   b. Phillis Wheatley
   c. Shirley Chisholm
   d. Marian Wright Edelman

3. Where was Martin Luther King, Jr. assassinated?
   a. Memphis, Tennessee
   b. Hartford, Connecticut
   c. Nashville, Tennessee
   d. Miami, Florida

4. How many men signed the Declaration of Independence?
   a. Forty-six
   b. Fifty-six
   c. Fifty
   d. One hundred

5. In 1917, the United States purchased the Virgin Islands from Denmark. How much did we pay?
   a. $1
   b. $1 million
   c. $10 million
   d. $25 million

6. What year was the five-digit Zip Code inaugurated?
   a. 1939
   b. 1953
   c. 1960
   d. 1963

7. What year was the Touch Tone phone introduced?
   a. 1944
   b. 1960
   c. 1963
   d. 1970

8. What was the name of the first communications satellite?
   a. Comsat 1
   b. Liberty
   c. Telstar
   d. BeamSat 1

9. How many Model Ts did the Ford Motor Company sell in the twenty years from its introduction in 1908 until the vehicle was discontinued in 1928?
   a. 200,000
   b. 2,000,000
   c. 10,000,000
   d. 15,000,000

10. Which Amendment to the Constitution permits an income tax?
    a. The Fifth
    b. The Sixteenth
    c. The Fourth
    d. The Twelfth

11. Which President was responsible for the program of economic and social reform known as The Great Society?
    a. Martin Van Buren
    b. Abraham Lincoln
    c. Lyndon Johnson
    d. Bill Clinton

12. Who was the first woman ever nominated for the office of Vice President?
    a. Sandra Day O'Connor
    b. Geraldine Ferraro
    c. Elizabeth Dole
    d. Christine Whitman

13. Who was known as "The Teflon President"?
    a. Bill Clinton   c. Jimmy Carter
    b. George Bush   d. Ronald Reagan

14. From the following list, identify the three American women who have appeared on United States currency.
    a. Eleanor Roosevelt   f. Virginia Dare
    b. Susan B. Anthony   g. Martha Washington
    c. Margaret Fuller   h. Harriet Tubman
    d. Hillary Rodham Clinton   i. Pocahantas
    e. Rosa Parks   j. Mary Harris "Mother" Jones

15. What percentage of the world's energy does the United States consume?
    a. 80 percent   c. 50 percent
    b. 24 percent   d. 10 percent

16. How many slaves were freed after the Civil War?
    a. 100,000   c. 4,000,000
    b. 1,000,000   d. 12,000,000

17. The Liberty Bell cracked when it was rung on July 8, 1835 in Philadephia. For what reason was the great bell rung that day?
    a. To commemorate the one-hundredth anniversary of the Georgia colony banning slavery
    b. To commemorate the two-hundredth anniversary of the Peace of Prague
    c. To announce the death of U.S. Supreme Court Justice John Marshall
    d. To celebrate the settlement of St. Petersburg, Florida

18. What branch of our government has authority over the Library of Congress, the Congressional Budget Office, the Architect of the Capitol, and the United States Botanic Garden?

a. The Legislative Branch   c. The Judicial Branch

b. The Executive Branch

19. TRUE OR FALSE: The Twenty-fourth Amendment to the Constitution prohibits poll taxes.

20. TRUE OR FALSE: *The New York Evening Post* was founded in 1801 by Benjamin Franklin.

21. TRUE OR FALSE: In 1987, the Supreme Court ruled in *Edwards v. Aguillard*, that Louisiana schools could teach creationism along with evolution.

22. Which of the following statements about slavery are FALSE?

a. The first recorded account of African slaves arriving in America was in 1619, in Jamestown, Virginia.

b. In 1661, Virginia passed legislation recognizing the legal existence of slavery.

c. In 1662, Virginia passed a law making slavery hereditary.

d. In 1670, a Massachusetts law stated that the offspring of slaves could be sold into slavery.

e. Slave ships transported Africans chained to shelves less than three feet apart.

f. One in six Africans died during the journey from Africa to the West Indies.

g. The international slave trade was terminated in America in 1807.

23. TRUE OR FALSE: In 1920, California passed a law prohibiting Japanese immigrants from leasing farmland in the state.

24. TRUE OR FALSE: AT&T introduced rotary telephone dialing in 1930.

25. TRUE OR FALSE: The First Amendment protects critics of public officials, even if the critics' charges and accusations against the official are false.

26. TRUE OR FALSE: Native Americans did not fight in World War I.

27. TRUE OR FALSE: King Gillette invented the safety razor in 1895.

28. TRUE OR FALSE: President Rutherford B. Hayes was known as "Tricky Dick."

29. TRUE OR FALSE: John F. Kennedy was the youngest President elected to the office.

30. TRUE OR FALSE: California was named for a fictitious earthly paradise mentioned in the sixteenth century romantic novel, *Las Serged de Esplandian.*

31. TRUE OR FALSE: The Department of Defense is part of the Judicial Branch of our government.

32. TRUE OR FALSE: In 1813, the Indian chief Tecumseh put a death curse on all U.S. Presidents elected in a year ending in a zero.

33. Place our forty-three Presidents in their proper order. Six Presidents have been filled in to get you started.

Abraham Lincoln	Harry S. Truman
Andrew Jackson	Herbert C. Hoover
Andrew Johnson	James A. Garfield
Benjamin Harrison	James Buchanan 15
Calvin Coolidge	James E. Carter, Jr.
Chester A. Arthur	James K. Polk
Dwight D. Eisenhower	James Madison
Franklin D. Roosevelt	James Monroe
Franklin Pierce	John Adams
George H. W. Bush 41	John F. Kennedy
George W. Bush 43	John Quincy Adams
George Washington 1	John Tyler
Gerald R. Ford	Lyndon B. Johnson
Grover Cleveland	Martin Van Buren 8
Grover Cleveland	Millard Fillmore

Richard M. Nixon

Ronald W. Reagan

Rutherford B. Hayes

Theodore Roosevelt

Thomas Jefferson

Ulysses S. Grant

Warren G. Harding

William Henry Harrison

William Howard Taft   27

William J. Clinton

William McKinley

Woodrow Wilson

Zachary Taylor

34. Place the original thirteen states in the correct order in which they were admitted to the Union:

Connecticut   ____

Delaware   ____

Georgia   ____

Maryland   ____

Massachusetts   ____

New Hampshire   ____

New Jersey   ____

New York   ____

North Carolina   ____

Pennsylvania   ____

Rhode Island   ____

South Carolina   ____

Virginia   ____

35. Place the following officeholders in the correct order of Presidential succession:

Attorney General   ____

President Pro Tempore of the Senate   ____

Secretary of Agriculture   ____

Secretary of Commerce   ____

Secretary of Defense   ____

Secretary of Education   ____

Secretary of Energy   ____

Secretary of Health and Human Services   ____

Secretary of Housing and Urban Development   ____

Secretary of Labor   ____

Secretary of State   ____

Secretary of the Interior   ____

Secretary of the Treasury   ____

Secretary of Transportation   ____

Speaker of the House   ____

Vice President   ____

36. The following paragraph is from a chapter called "My First Campaign" from a book written by a former U. S. President. Identify the President and his book.

"When I was at the U.S. Naval Academy and later on ships, my duties took me to Washington every now and then, and I always visited our Georgia Congressman Carl Vinson, who was chairman of the House Committee on Naval Affairs, and the Senate chambers where Senators Walter F. George and Richard B. Russell served. Senator Russell, as chairman of the Armed Services Commitee, was especially interested in the Navy's new programs which, on a few occasions, I had a chance to discuss with him. After I joined the nuclear submarine program, I went to Washington more frequently to meet with my boss, Admiral Hyman Rickover. All of us had watched the political developments closely in 1952, when Admiral Rickover was almost forced out of the Navy by conservative senior officers and was saved only by the strong actions of President Harry Truman and congressional leaders, including my fellow Georgians."

37. The first person to sign the Declaration of Independence was John _____.

38. SALT stands for Strategic _____ Limitation _____.

39. TRUE OR FALSE: Lieutenant William L. Calley was sentenced to life in prison for the March 16, 1968, slaughter of 347 South Vietnamese villagers known as the My Lai Incident.

40. TRUE OR FALSE: Lieutenant William L. Calley is in prison today.

41. The militant black political party founded in 1966 by Huey Newton was known as the _____ _____.

42. The 1777–1778 winter headquarters of General George Washington and his troops was _____ _____, _____.

43. This 1964 Resolution gave the President the power "to take all necessary measures to repel any armed attack against the United States and to prevent further aggression." This Resolution resulted in the escalation of the Vietnam War.

44. In 1867, the United States purchased Alaska. From what country did we buy the territory, and how much did we pay for it?

45. Name the five most populated states in the Union, in order from most populated.

46. Name the five least populated states in the Union, in order from least populated.

47. What do the following men all have in common?: Charles Conrad, Jr.; Alan Bean; Alan Shephard, Jr.; Edgar Mitchell; David Scott; James Irwin; John Young; Charles Duke, Jr.; Eugene Cernan; Harrison Schmitt.

48. Name the place "where America's day begins."

49. What do the following men all have in common? Elbridge Gerry, Millard Fillmore, Schuyler Colfax, Levi Morton, and Richard Nixon.

50. What was the first country to recognize the United States as an independent country, and in what year did this country publicly acknowledge the U.S.'s independent status?

51. TRUE OR FALSE: The flag at the White House is flown every day of the year, twenty-four hours a day, year-round.

52. When was the phrase "under God" added to the Pledge of Allegiance by Congress?

53. What are the only two flags that may be flown *above* the United States flag?
    a. The flag of the United Nations
    b. The flag of the Pope
    c. A Navy chaplain's church pennant
    d. The flag of any other country

54. Name the first two states admitted to the Union *after* the original thirteen colonies were admitted.

55. Everyone knows that Alaska and Hawaii were the last two states admitted to the Union. Alaska, number forty-nine, in 1959; and Hawaii, number fifty, in 1960. Name the two states admitted to the Union immediately *before* Alaska and Hawaii. (**Hint:** States forty-seven and forty-eight were both admitted to the Union on July 4, 1912.)

56. What ritual concerning the U.S. flag is officially observed each year on Memorial Day?
    a. The flag is never officially flown on Memorial Day.

    b. The flag is flown at half-staff until noon on Memorial Day.

    c. The flag is not flown at the United Nations or over foreign embassies on Memorial Day.

    d. The flag is only flown over official military cemeteries on Memorial Day.

57. Only two people actually signed the Declaration of Independence on July 4, 1776: John Hancock and one other person. Name this other person.

58. What was the first state to secede from the Union during the Civil War?

59. The office of President of the United States as we know it was created in the Constitution written in 1787. However, prior to George Washington, fourteen other men had held the title of President, although they were technically known as President of Congress. Name the first man to officially carry the title of "President" in America.

60. Name the only U.S. President buried in Washington, D.C.

61. As of July 4, 2004, how many American Presidents were still living?

62. One state has been the birthplace of more Presidents—eight—than any other state. Name this state *and* the Presidents born there.

63. Name the document in which the following Article can be found: "The parties agree that an armed attack against one or more of them in Europe or North America shall be considered an attack against them all."

64. Who said, "I know not what course others may take, but as for me, give me liberty or give me death" and when and where did he say it?

65. In 1889, a great American steel magnate (who died in 1919) published an article in the *North American Review* called "Wealth" in which he put forth the then-shocking and never-before considered notion that the rich had a duty to use their surplus wealth for the betterment of society. Who was this important industrialist?

66. What great civil rights leader once described the Vietnam War as "one of history's most cruel and senseless wars"?

67. TRUE OR FALSE: Walt Disney served as a Red Cross ambulance driver during World War I.

68. What was Mickey Mouse's original name?
    a. Mikey Mouse
    b. Mortimer Mouse
    c. Miggsy Mouse
    d. Mousey Mouse
    e. Mickey Mouse was the original name Walt Disney came up with for his beloved animated rodent.

69. Name President Lincoln's Secretary of State; the man who not only purchased Alaska from Russia but who was also attacked by a co-conspirator of John Wilkes Booth, President Lincoln's assassin.

70. Who was elected President of the Republic of Texas in September 1836?

71. TRUE OR FALSE: Alexander Graham Bell (3/3/1847–8/2/1922) was born in the Bronx.

72. What was Satchmo's real name?

73. What famous female suffragette and recipient of the 1931 Nobel Peace Prize published her autobiography—*Twenty Years at Hull House*—in 1919?

74. What famous printer, author, statesman, diplomat, scientist, and philanthropist invented bifocal glasses at the age of eighty-three?

75. This famous poet and short story writer died from alcohol and opiates in Baltimore in 1849 at the age of forty. Following his death, the French poet Charles Baudelaire translated his writings into French, resulting in his becoming the first American author to be widely read and passionately admired in France. Name this American writer.

76. What famous aviator made the first solo airplane flight from Honolulu, Hawaii to the U.S. mainland, as well as the first nonstop flight from Mexico City to Newark, New Jersey?

77. TRUE OR FALSE: An American has never been named a Secretary-General of the United Nations.

78. TRUE OR FALSE: Guam's roads are made of ground coral because the island has no sand.

79. What was the name of the U.S. administrative body that, in April, 1942, stopped all construction in America that was not essential to the war effort?

80. What is the name of the official military periodical?

QUIZ 85

American Lasts

☆ ☆ ☆ ☆ ☆

1. On July 26, 1951, the U.S. Army officially disbanded the Twenty-fourth Infantry Regiment, the last unit of its kind. What was unique about the Twenty-fourth Infantry Regiment?

2. What two teams played the last game at Ebbetts Field in Brooklyn before it was demolished to build apartment houses?

3. TRUE OR FALSE: The last public execution in the United States—a hanging—occurred in Kentucky on August 14, 1936.

4. What was the last film to be condemned by the Legion of Decency, the Catholic committee made up of U.S. bishops, before it was disbanded and renamed the National Catholic Office for Motion Pictures?

   a. Ingmar Bergman's *The Silence*, for "vulgar" images

   b. Roman Polanski's *Knife in the Water*, for nudity

   c. Richard Brooks's *Cat on a Hot Tin Roof*, for homosexual references

   d. Sidney Lumet's *The Pawnbroker*, for showing a woman's breasts

5. What was the subject of FDR's last "fireside chat," which he delivered on June 23, 1944?

   a. It was a report on the progress of World War II and a discussion of the need for Americans to continue to support the war effort.

   b. It was a tirade against "shortsighted" Republicans.

   c. It was a reminiscence of his childhood days.

   d. It was a warm appreciation of his wife.

6. Who was the last President to live in the White House without electricity?
   a. James Garfield
   b. Chester A. Arthur
   c. Grover Cleveland
   d. Benjamin Harrison

7. What was veteran actor Lionel Barrymore's last film role?
   a. *Dinner at Eight*
   b. He played himself in a cameo role in *Main Street to Broadway* in 1953.
   c. *Bannerline*
   d. *Down to the Sea in Ships*

8. What was the name of the U.S. venue where the Beatles performed their last concert?

9. What was the last major battle of the Civil War?
   a. The Battle of Mobile Bay, Alabama
   b. The Battle of Fort Fisher, North Carolina
   c. The Battle at Five Forks, Virginia
   d. Sayler's Creek, Virginia

10. What is the last word of the U.S. Pledge of Allegiance?

PRESIDENTIAL REFERENCE APPENDIX

The Presidents of the United States

☆ ☆ ☆ ☆ ☆

	PRESIDENT	TERM	BIRTH	DEATH
1.	George Washington	1789–1797	February 22, 1732	December 14, 1799
2.	John Adams	1797–1801	October 30, 1735	July 4, 1826
3.	Thomas Jefferson	1801–1809	April 13, 1743	July 4, 1826
4.	James Madison	1809–1817	March 16, 1751	June 28, 1836
5.	James Monroe	1817–1825	April 28, 1758	July 4, 1831
6.	John Quincy Adams	1825–1829	July 11, 1767	February 23, 1848
7.	Andrew Jackson	1829–1837	March 15, 1767	June 8, 1845
8.	Martin Van Buren	1837–1841	December 5, 1782	July 24, 1862
9.	William Henry Harrison	1841	February 9, 1773	April 4, 1841
10.	John Tyler	1841–1845	March 29, 1790	January 18, 1862
11.	James Polk	1845–1849	November 2, 1795	June 15, 1849
12.	Zachary Taylor	1849–1850	November 24, 1784	July 9, 1850
13.	Millard Fillmore	1850–1853	January 7, 1800	March 8, 1874
14.	Franklin Pierce	1853–1857	November 23, 1804	October 8, 1869
15.	James Buchanan	1857–1861	April 23, 1791	June 1, 1868
16.	Abraham Lincoln	1861–1865	February 12, 1809	April 15, 1865
17.	Andrew Johnson	1865–1869	December 29, 1808	July 31, 1875
18.	Ulysses S. Grant	1869–1877	April 27, 1822	July 23, 1885
19.	Rutherford B. Hayes	1877–1881	October 4, 1822	January 17, 1893
20.	James Garfield	1881	November 19, 1831	September 19, 1881
21.	Chester A. Arthur	1881–1885	October 5, 1829	November 18, 1886

PRESIDENT	TERM	BIRTH	DEATH
22. Grover Cleveland	1885–1889	March 18, 1837	June 24, 1908
23. Benjamin Harrison	1889–1893	August 20, 1833	March 13, 1901
24. Grover Cleveland	1893–1897	March 18, 1837	June 24, 1908
25. William McKinley	1897–1901	January 29, 1843	September 14, 1901
26. Theodore Roosevelt	1901–1909	October 27, 1858	January 6, 1919
27. William Howard Taft	1909–1913	September 15, 1857	March 8, 1930
28. Woodrow Wilson	1913–1921	December 28, 1856	February 3, 1924
29. Warren G. Harding	1921–1923	November 2, 1865	August 2, 1923
30. Calvin Coolidge	1923–1929	July 4, 1872	January 5, 1933
31. Herbert Hoover	1929–1933	August 10, 1874	October 20, 1964
32. Franklin D. Roosevelt	1933–1945	January 30, 1882	April 12, 1945
33. Harry S. Truman	1945–1953	May 8, 1884	December 26, 1972
34. Dwight D. Eisenhower	1953–1961	October 14, 1890	March 28, 1969
35. John F. Kennedy	1961–1963	May 29, 1917	November 22, 1963
36. Lyndon B. Johnson	1963–1969	August 27, 1908	January 22, 1973
37. Richard Nixon	1969–1974	January 9, 1913	April 22, 1994
38. Gerald Ford	1974–1977	July 14, 1913	
39. Jimmy Carter	1977–1981	October 1, 1924	
40. Ronald Reagan	1981–1989	February 6, 1911	
41. George Bush	1989–1993	June 12, 1924	
42. Bill Clinton	1993–2001	August 19, 1946	
43. George W. Bush	2001–200?	July 6, 1946	

Answers

Quiz 1: Coming to America: The Immigration Experience

1. Believe it or not, this is all true. U.S. citizenship was required for all these professions. (**Note:** Twenty-six out of the forty-eight states required citizenship to become a lawyer; in twelve other states, court rulings made citizenship mandatory for admission to the bar in these states.)

2. b.

3. England.

4. Ellis Island is an island in the upper New York Bay, southwest of Manhattan.

5. True.

6. d.

7. Currently, Green Cards are blue, pink, and white. They are called Green Cards because they actually were green when the U.S. government first started issuing them after World War II. They are now called "Permanent Resident Cards" but everyone automatically uses the term "Green Card" when referring to the ID card needed by all immigrants who wish to live and work in the United States.

8. <u>Three</u> percent. So, if 500,000 people who had been born in Spain were living in the United States in 1910, the maximum number of immigrants from Spain allowed into the U.S. in 1922 would be 15,000. Convoluted, yes, but that was the formula used until the Immigration Act of 1924 was passed, which lowered the percentage to 2 percent.

9. c.

10. d.

Quiz 2: Which President . . . ?

1. a. Lincoln was 6′ 4″ tall; Johnson was 6′ 3″; Jefferson was 6′ 2.5″; and Clinton is 6′ 2″.

2. e. JFK was not a Mason. All the others were Masons, in addition to James Monroe, Andrew Jackson, James Polk, Andrew Johnson, William McKinley, Theodore Roosevelt, William Howard Taft, Warren Harding, Franklin Delano Roosevelt, and Harry Truman.

3. c. Grover Cleveland did not die in office. In addition to the four Presidents listed who did, four other Presidents died in office: Abraham Lincoln, William McKinley, Warren Harding, and Franklin Delano Roosevelt.

4. d. Van Buren was the first U.S. President not born a British subject. Eight U.S. Presidents were born British subjects even though they were in North America at the time. In addition to the four listed, John Adams, James Madison, John Quincy Adams, and Andrew Jackson were also born British subjects.

5. a. JFK was the first Roman Catholic elected President.

6. d.

7. b.

8. a.

9. e. Andrew Jackson was a bigamist. When he married Rachel Robards in 1791, her divorce from her first husband had not been finalized and she was still married. When this was discovered, Jackson had to re-marry her after she was divorced.

10. a.

11. c, d. The term used was "indentured servant," but the reality was that indentured servants were little more than slaves who had to buy their freedom in order to be let go.

12. b. Buchanan's niece Harriet served as White House hostess during his administration.

13. b.

14. d.

15. d.

16. d. The ceremony took place in 1922.

17. a.

18. e.

19. d.

20. b. President Carter added to the insult by referring to his problem as "Montezuma's Revenge," which is perceived by Mexicans as a Yankee slur.

Quiz 3: Presidential Milestones

1,v; 2,mm; 3,nn; 4,bb; 5,oo; 6,i; 7,ll; 8,y; 9,x; 10,n; 11,pp; 12,kk; 13,h; 14,jj; 15,o; 16,d; 17,w; 18,z; 19,ff; 20,q; 21,t; 22,u; 23,s; 24,ee; 25,r; 26,e; 27,cc; 28,l; 29,hh; 30,g; 31,f; 32,b; 33,aa; 34,dd; 35,gg; 36,j; 37,qq; 38,k; 39,p; 40,a; 41,c; 42,ii; 43,m.

Quiz 4: The Presidents and Their Wars

1,j; 2,a; 3,g; 4,b; 5,l; 6,d; 7,c; 8,e; 9,m; 10,i; 11,h; 12,f; 13,k.

Quiz 5: On the Road Again

1. Calvin Coolidge.
2. Dwight D. Eisenhower.
3. Franklin Delano Roosevelt.
4. George Bush.
5. George W. Bush.
6. Gerald Ford.
7. Harry S. Truman.
8. Jimmy Carter.
9. John F. Kennedy.
10. Lyndon B. Johnson.
11. Richard Nixon.
12. Ronald Reagan.
13. Theodore Roosevelt.
14. Bill Clinton.
15. Herbert Hoover.

Quiz 6: Presidential Pens

1,s; 2,g; 3,v; 4,a; 5,d; 6,n; 7,q; 8,b; 9,o; 10,c; 11,l; 12,u; 13,e; 14,j; 15,f; 16,t; 17,h; 18,i; 19,r; 20,p; 21,k; 22,m.

Quiz 7: Last Words

1. "Doctor, I am going. Perhaps it is best." <u>John Tyler.</u>
2. "Good-bye. Good-bye to all. It is God's will. His will, not ours, be done." <u>William McKinley.</u>
3. "I am a broken piece of machinery. When the machinery is broken . . . I am ready." <u>Woodrow Wilson.</u>
4. "I am about to die. I expect the summons very soon. I have tried to discharge my duties faithfully. I regret nothing, but I am sorry that I am about to leave my friends." <u>Zachary Taylor.</u>
5. "I am just going. Have me decently buried and do not let my body be put into a vault in less than two days after I am dead. Do you understand me? 'Tis well." <u>George Washington.</u>
6. "I have a terrific headache" <u>Franklin Delano Roosevelt.</u>

7. "I have tried so hard to do right." <u>Grover Cleveland.</u>

8. "I know that I am going where Lucy is." <u>Rutherford B. Hayes.</u>

9. "I want to go; God take me." <u>Dwight D. Eisenhower.</u>

10. "I wish you to understand the true principles of the Government. I wish them carried out. I ask nothing more." <u>William Henry Harrison.</u>

11. "Is it the Fourth?" <u>Thomas Jefferson.</u>

12. "Nothing more than a change of *mind*, my dear." <u>James Madison.</u>

13. "Oh, do not cry. Be good children, and we shall all meet in Heaven." <u>Andrew Jackson.</u>

14. "Please put out the light." <u>Theodore Roosevelt.</u>

15. "Swaim, can't you stop this? Oh, Swaim!" <u>James A. Garfield.</u>

16. "That is very obvious." <u>John F. Kennedy.</u>

17. "That's good. Go on; read some more." <u>Warren G. Harding.</u>

18. "This is the end of earth," followed by either, "but I am composed" or, "I am content." <u>John Quincy Adams.</u>

19. "Thomas Jefferson still survives." <u>John Adams.</u>

20. "Water." <u>Ulysses S. Grant.</u>

Detailed Explanations and Notes

- George Washington (First President): "I am just going. Have me decently buried and do not let my body be put into a vault in less than two days after I am dead. Do you understand me? 'Tis well." December 14, 1799, sometime after 10:00 P.M.

- John Adams (Second President): "Thomas Jefferson still survives."[a] July 4, 1826, around 6:00 P.M.

- Thomas Jefferson (Third President): "Is it the Fourth?" July 4, 1826, 12:50 P.M.

- James Madison (Fourth President): "Nothing more than a change of *mind*, my dear." June 28, 1836, sometime after 6:00 A.M.

- John Quincy Adams (Sixth President): "This is the end of earth," followed by either, "but I am composed" or "I am content." February 23, 1848, 7:20 P.M.

- Andrew Jackson (Seventh President): "Oh, do not cry. Be good children, and we shall all meet in Heaven." June 8, 1845, around 6:00 P.M.

- William Henry Harrison (Ninth President): "I wish you to understand the true principles of the Government. I wish them carried out. I ask nothing more." April 4, 1841, 12:30 A.M.

- John Tyler (Tenth President): "Doctor, I am going. Perhaps it is best." January 18, 1862, 12:15 A.M.

- Zachary Taylor (Twelfth President): "I am about to die. I expect the summons very soon. I have tried to discharge my duties faithfully. I regret nothing, but I am sorry that I am about to leave my friends." July 9, 1850, 10:35 P.M.

- Ulysses S. Grant (Eighteenth President): "Water." July 23, 1885, around 8:00 A.M.

- Rutherford B. Hayes (Nineteenth President): "I know that I am going where Lucy is."[b] January 17, 1893, 11:00 P.M.

- James A. Garfield (Twentieth President): "Swaim, can't you stop this? Oh, Swaim!"[c] July 2, 1881, 9:30 A.M. (Assassinated.)

- Grover Cleveland (Twenty-second and Twenty-fourth President): "I have tried so hard to do right." June 24, 1908, 8:40 P.M.

- William McKinley (Twenty-fifth President): "Good-bye. Good-bye to all. It is God's will. His will, not ours, be done." September 6, 1901, 4:07 P.M.

- Theodore Roosevelt (Twenty-sixth President): "Please put out the light." January 6, 1919, shortly after 4:00 A.M.

- Woodrow Wilson (Twenty-eighth President): "I am a broken piece of machinery. When the machinery is broken . . . I am ready." February 3, 1924, 11:15 A.M.

- Warren G. Harding (Twenty-ninth President): "That's good. Go on; read some more."[d] August 2, 1923, 7:23 P.M.

- Franklin D. Roosevelt (Thirty-second President): "I have a terrific headache."[e] April 12, 1945, 3:35 P.M.

- Dwight D. Eisenhower (Thirty-fourth President): "I want to go; God take me." March 28, 1969, 12:35 P.M.

- John F. Kennedy (Thirty-fifth President): "That is very obvious."[f] November 22, 1963, 12:30 P.M. (Assassinated.)

[a] In one of most astonishing coincidences of American history, John Adams and Thomas Jefferson—the two signers of the Declaration of Independence to become United States Presidents—both died on the same day, July 4, 1826—the fiftieth anniversary of the Declaration of Independence. Ironically, when Adams uttered his final declaration, he did not know that Jefferson had died around five hours earlier.

[b] Lucy was President Hayes's deceased wife.

[c] Swaim was President Garfield's physician and Garfield was asking him if he could stop the pain he was suffering.

ᵈ Mrs. Harding was reading aloud to the President an article called "A Calm View of a Calm Man" from the *Saturday Evening Post*, which was about Harding and which was a very positive and complimentary profile.

ᵉ When he said this, FDR had just suffered what would ultimately be a fatal cerebral hemorrhage.

ᶠ JFK said this in response to a comment Mrs. Connally (the Texas governor's wife) said to the President. "Mr. President," she remarked, "you can't say Dallas doesn't love you."

Quiz 8: Presidential Nicknames

1. George Washington: u, iii.
2. John Adams: b.
3. Thomas Jefferson: t.
4. James Madison: ccc.
5. James Monroe: rr.
6. John Quincy Adams: kkk, g.
7. Andrew Jackson: m, s.
8. Martin Van Buren: q, qq, aaa.
9. William Henry Harrison: fff.
10. John Tyler: z.
11. James K. Polk: ff.
12. Zachary Taylor: h.
13. Millard Fillmore: i.
14. Franklin Pierce: c.
15. James Buchanan: pp.
16. Abraham Lincoln: e.
17. Andrew Johnson: kk.
18. Ulysses S. Grant: vv, ww, lll.
19. Rutherford B. Hayes: d.
20. James A. Garfield: dd.
21. Chester A. Arthur: jjj.
22. Grover Cleveland: a, f, l, hhh.
23. Benjamin Harrison: ddd.
24. William McKinley: o, ggg.
25. Theodore Roosevelt: j, k, cc, eee.
26. William Howard Taft: n.
27. Woodrow Wilson: ss, bbb.
28. Warren G. Harding: ii.
29. Calvin Coolidge: jj.
30. Herbert C. Hoover: zz.
31. Franklin D. Roosevelt: p, r, aa, ee, xx, yy.
32. Harry S. Truman: x.
33. Dwight D. Eisenhower: uu.
34. John F. Kennedy: v.
35. Lyndon B. Johnson: gg.
36. Richard M. Nixon: w, tt.
37. Gerald Ford: oo.
38. Jimmy Carter: nn.
39. Ronald Reagan: y, hh.
40. George Bush: bb.
41. William Jefferson Clinton: mm.
42. George W. Bush: ll.

Quiz 9: Presidential Burial Places

1. George Washington, t.
2. John Adams, aa.
3. Thomas Jefferson, f.
4. James Madison, s.
5. James Monroe, bb.
6. John Quincy Adams, aa.
7. Andrew Jackson, u.
8. Martin Van Buren, o.
9. William Henry Harrison, w.
10. John Tyler, bb.
11. James K. Polk, u.
12. Zachary Taylor, q.
13. Millard Fillmore, d.
14. Franklin Pierce, h.
15. James Buchanan, p.
16. Abraham Lincoln, cc.
17, Andrew Johnson, j.
18. Ulysses S. Grant, v.
19. Rutherford B. Hayes, i.
20. James A. Garfield, g.
21. Chester A. Arthur, b.
22. Grover Cleveland, z.
23. Benjamin Harrison, m.
24. William McKinley, e.
25. Theodore Roosevelt, x.
26. William Howard Taft, c.
27. Woodrow Wilson, dd.
28. Warren G. Harding, r.
29. Calvin Coolidge, y.
30. Herbert C. Hoover, ee.
31. Franklin D. Roosevelt, k.
32. Harry S. Truman, l.
33. Dwight D. Eisenhower, a.
34. John F. Kennedy, c.
35. Lyndon B. Johnson, n.
36. Richard M. Nixon, ff.

Quiz 10: Our American Government: Part 1

1. The United States, under its Constitution, is a federal, representative, democratic republic, an indivisible union of fifty sovereign States. With the exception of town meetings, a form of pure democracy, we have at the local, state, and national levels a government which is: "federal" because power is shared among those three levels; "democratic" because the people govern themselves and have the means to control the government; and "republic" because the people choose elected delegates by free and secret ballot.

2. Some of the U.S. contributions to the institution of government are as follows: a written constitution, an independent judiciary to interpret the Constitution, and a division of powers between the Federal and state governments.

3. The framers of the Constitution debated and agreed to the following six basic principles:

   1. That all States would be equal. The National Government cannot give special privileges to one State.

   2. That there should be three branches of Government—one to make the laws, another to execute them, and a third to interpret them.

   3. That the Government is a government of laws, not of men. No one is above the law. No officer of the Government can use authority unless and except as the Constitution or public law permits.

   4. That all men are equal before the law and that anyone, rich or poor, can demand the protection of the law.

   5. That the people can change the authority of the Government by changing (amending) the Constitution. (One such change provided for the election of Senators by direct popular vote instead of by State legislatures.)

   6. That the Constitution, and the laws of the United States and treaties made pursuant to it, are "the supreme Law of the Land."

4. Amending the Constitution involves two separate processes.

   First, amendments may be proposed on the initiative of Congress (by two-thirds affirmative vote in each House) or by convention (on application of two-thirds of the State legislatures). So far, a convention has never been called.

   The second step is ratification of a proposed amendment. At the discretion of Congress, Congress may designate ratification either by the State legislatures or by conventions. Ratification requires approval by three-fourths of the States. Out of the twenty-seven amendments, only one (the Twenty-first, ending Prohibition) has been ratified by State conventions.

   The first ten amendments (ratified in 1791) were practically a part of the original instrument. The Eleventh Amendment was ratified in 1795, and the Twelfth Amendment in 1804. Thereafter, no amendment was made to the Constitution for sixty years. Shortly after the Civil War, three amendments were ratified (1865–70), followed by another long interval before the Sixteenth Amendment became effective in 1913. The most recent amendment, the Twenty-seventh, was ratified on May 7, 1992. At the present time, there are four amendments pending before the States that were proposed without ratification deadlines.

5. The "lame duck" amendment is the popular name for the Twentieth Amendment to the Constitution, ratified on February 6, 1933. It is designed to limit the time that elected officials can serve after the general election in November. This amendment provides, among other things, that the terms of the President and Vice President end at noon on January 20,

the terms of Senators and Representatives end at noon on January 3, and the terms of their successors then begin.

Prior to this amendment, the annual session of Congress began on the first Monday in December (Article 1, Section 4). Since the terms of new members formerly did not begin until March 4, Members who had been defeated or did not stand for reelection in November continued to serve during the lame duck session from December until March 4. Adoption of the Twentieth Amendment has reduced but not eliminated legislation by a Congress that does not represent the latest choice of the people. For instance, eleven of the thirty-three Congresses from 1933 to 1999 (73rd through the 105th Congress) continued to meet after the November general elections.

Quiz 11: Our American Government: Part 2

1. The "separation of powers" and "checks and balances" are two fundamental principles underlying the Constitution. They work together to prevent a tyrannous concentration of power in any one branch, to check and restrain Government, and, ultimately, to protect the rights and liberties of citizens.

   The Constitution contains provisions in separate articles for the three branches of Government—legislative, executive, and judicial. There is a significant difference in the grants of authority to these branches, each of which is also given an independent base of political power. The First Article, dealing with legislative power, vests in Congress "all legislative powers herein granted"; the Second Article vests "the executive Power" in the President; and the Third Article states that "The judicial power of the United States shall be vested in one Supreme Court, and in such inferior Courts as the Congress may from time to time ordain and establish." In addition to this separation and independence among the three branches, the Constitution sets up "auxiliary precautions," as James Madison called them in the Federalist Papers, that allow each branch to check and balance the others. For instance, the President can veto bills approved by Congress and nominate individuals to the Federal judiciary; the Supreme Court can declare a law enacted by Congress or an action by the President unconstitutional; and Congress can impeach and remove the President and Federal court justices and judges.

2. The officers and senior officials of the House are, except where noted, elected by the House at the beginning of each Congress. They are the principal managers for the House of essential legislative, financial, administrative, and security functions. Their duties are prescribed in House Rule II and in statutes.

   The Clerk of the House: The Clerk is the chief legislative officer of the House. After each election, the Clerk receives the credentials of newly elected Members and presides at the opening of each new Congress pending the election of a Speaker. The Clerk keeps the official Journal of House proceedings, certifies all votes, and signs all bills and resolutions that have passed the House. The Clerk's office supervises legislative information resources in the House, the page program, and units providing public documents to the press and public.

The Sergeant at Arms: The Sergeant at Arms is responsible for maintaining order on the floor and in the galleries when the House is in session. The office also maintains security in the House side of the Capitol and in House office buildings and facilities. As part of this responsibility, the Sergeant at Arms, along with his or her Senate counterpart and the Architect of the Capitol, comprise the Capitol Police Board and the Capitol Guide Board. In addition, the Sergeant at Arms is charged with carrying out Section 5 of Article I of the Constitution, which authorizes the House (and Senate) "to compel the Attendance of absent Members."

The Chaplain: The House Chaplain opens each daily House session with a prayer and provides pastoral services to House Members, their families, and staff. He also arranges for visits by guest chaplains. Traditionally, the Chaplain retains his post when party control of the House changes.

The Chief Administrative Officer (CAO): The CAO is the principal House officer responsible for the financial management of House of Representatives accounts. Quarterly, his office issues a public document identifying all expenditures made by House Members, committees, and officers from appropriated funds at their disposal. The CAO's office, in addition to its financial management responsibilities, provides a range of services to Member and committee offices, including telecommunications, postal, and computer services, office supply and maintenance services, payroll and accounting services, employee counseling and assistance programs, and supervises private vendors and contractors providing services to the House.

The Inspector General (IG): The Inspector General is the chief investigative officer of the House. His office (either through its own staff or through consultants) conducts periodic audits of House financial and administrative offices and operations. The IG's findings and recommendations are submitted to the appropriate House offices, to the congressional leadership, and to the House Administration Committee. The IG serves a two-year term and is jointly appointed by the Speaker, the Majority Leader, and the Minority Leader.

The General Counsel: The General Counsel is the chief legal advisor to the House, its leaders and officers, and to its Members. The office represents the House, its Members, or employees in litigation resulting from the performance of official duties. The General Counsel is appointed by the Speaker in consultation with a bipartisan legal advisory group, which includes the Majority and Minority leaders.

The Historian: By statute, the Office of the Historian acts to preserve the historical records of the House and its Members, to encourage historical research on the House, and to undertake original research and writing on the history of the House. The Historian is appointed by the Speaker. When the post is vacant, other legislative branch organizations and offices may perform some of these services and functions.

3. The Constitution provides that "the Vice President of the United States shall be the President of the Senate" (Article 1, section 3). As President of the Senate, the Vice President presides over the Senate, makes parliamentary rulings (which may be overturned by a majority vote of the Senate), and may cast tie-breaking votes. At first, Vice Presidents presided on a regular basis, but in recent years they are present in the chair only when a close vote is anticipated, during major debates, or on important ceremonial occasions (such as the swearing in of newly elected Senators, or during joint sessions). In the absence of the Vice President, the Senate elects a President pro tempore (president "for the time being") to preside. In recent decades it has become traditional for this post to go to the senior Senator from the majority party. The President pro tempore assigns other Members of the majority party to preside by rotation during each day's proceedings. These Senators and the President pro tempore retain their rights to vote on all issues before the body and to debate when they are not presiding.

4. The political parties in the House and Senate elect Leaders to represent them on the floor, to advocate their policies and viewpoints, to coordinate their legislative efforts, and to help determine the schedule of legislative business. The Leaders serve as spokespersons for their parties and for the House and Senate as a whole. Since the Framers of the Constitution did not anticipate political parties, these leadership posts are not defined in the Constitution but have evolved over time. The House, with its larger membership, required Majority and Minority Leaders in the nineteenth century to expedite legislative business and to keep their parties united. The Senate did not formally designate party floor leaders until the 1920s, although several caucus chairmen and committee chairmen had previously performed similar duties. In both Houses, the parties also elect assistant leaders, or "Whips." The Majority Leader is elected by the majority-party conference (or caucus), the Minority Leader by the minority-party conference. Third parties have rarely had enough members to need to elect their own leadership, and independents will generally join one of the larger party organizations to receive committee assignments. Majority and Minority Leaders receive a higher salary than other Members in recognition of their additional responsibilities.

5. The congressional budget process, established by the Congressional Budget and Impoundment Control Act of 1974, is the means by which Congress develops and enforces an overall budgetary plan, including levels for total revenues, total spending, and a surplus or deficit. This blueprint for all Federal spending is established in the form of a concurrent resolution on the budget. Spending authority is then allocated to congressional committees pursuant to this resolution. The rules of both the House and Senate prohibit spending measures in excess of these allocations. Any changes in existing law that are necessary to achieve these targets can be enacted in the form of a reconciliation bill.

Quiz 12: Our American Government: Part 3

1. Authorizations and appropriations are separate and distinct parts of the Federal budget process. Authorizations are measures which establish Federal policies and programs, and may also make recommendations concerning the proper spending level for a program or agency. Those recommendations are acted upon in the form of appropriations, which provide specific dollar amounts for agencies, programs, and operations. If an authorization specifies a spending level or upper limit, this amount acts as the maximum that an appropriation can provide. The rules of both the House and the Senate prohibit unauthorized appropriations, but both Chambers have developed practices to avoid the operation of these rules if it is the desire of the Chamber to do so.

2. In addition to Congress—the House of Representatives and the Senate— the legislative branch includes the Architect of the Capitol, the Government Printing Office (GPO), the Library of Congress, and the legislative support agencies. The Architect's principal duties involve the construction, maintenance, and renovation of the Capitol Building as well as the congressional office buildings and other structures in the Capitol complex such as the Library of Congress buildings. GPO publishes the Congressional Record, congressional committee hearings and reports, and other congressional documents, as well as many executive branch publications. The Library of Congress, in addition to providing library services, research, and analysis to Congress, is also the national library. It houses premier national book, map, and manuscript collections in the United States; serves a major role assisting local libraries in book cataloging and other services; and supervises the implementation of U.S. copyright laws.

Three support agencies are also part of the legislative branch. The Congressional Budget Office, the Congressional Research Service in the Library of Congress, and the General Accounting Office directly assist Congress in the performance of its duties. On occasion, temporary advisory commissions are established and funded in the legislative branch.

3. The Constitution gives to Congress the authority to declare war; this has occurred on only five occasions since 1789, the most recent being World War II. But the President, as Commander in Chief, has implied powers to commit the Nation's military forces, which has occurred on more than two hundred occasions in U.S. history. Moreover, Congress may authorize the use of the military in specific cases through public law.

The War Powers Resolution, enacted on November 7, 1973, as Public Law 93–148, also tried to clarify these respective roles of the President and Congress in cases involving the use of armed forces without a declaration of war. The President is expected to consult with Congress before using the armed forces "in every possible instance," and is required to report to Congress within forty-eight hours of introducing troops. Use of the armed forces is to be terminated within sixty days, with a possible thirty-day extension by the President, unless Congress acts during that time to declare war, enacts a specific authorization for use of the armed forces, extends the sixty to ninety day period, or is physically unable to meet as a result of an attack on the United States.

4. Simply as "Mr. President." A letter sent to the Chief Executive is addressed "The President, The White House."

One of the earliest congressional debates dealt with the title of the Chief Executive. A committee of the House of Representatives suggested the simple title "The President of the United States." However, the Senate rejected this report in May 1789 at the behest of Vice President John Adams. Adams believed that "titles and politically inspired elegance were essential aspects of strong government," and supported the title "His Highness the President of the United States and protector of their Liberties." George Washington himself was annoyed by this debate and made known his annoyance at Adams's attempts to "bedizen him with a superb but spurious title." The issue was resolved on May 27 when the Senate agreed that the Chief Executive should have the simple title "the President of the United States."

5. The oath of office for the President is prescribed by Article II, section 1, clause 8 of the Constitution as follows: I do solemnly swear (or affirm) that I will faithfully execute the office of President of the United States, and will, to the best of my ability, preserve, protect, and defend the Constitution of the United States.

Usually, the Chief Justice of the Supreme Court administers the oath, although there is no provision made for this within the Constitution. In fact, other judges have administered the oath at times of unexpected presidential succession.

6. In the event that the President-elect dies or resigns after the electoral vote is cast, then the Vice President-elect would be sworn in as President, as provided for in the Twentieth Amendment.

7. The guiding principle of the U.S. system of justice, "Equal Justice Under Law," is engraved in the marble pediment above the entrance of the U.S. Supreme Court Building.

8. Article VI of the Constitution provides that the Constitution and the laws of the United States made "in Pursuance thereof" shall be the supreme law of the land. Thus, when the Supreme Court decides a case, particularly on constitutional grounds, it becomes guidance for all the lower courts and legislators when a similar question arises. Under its power of judicial review, the Court can declare laws unconstitutional, thus making them null and void.

9. Candidates may spend unlimited amounts of their own personal funds on their campaigns, except Presidential and Vice Presidential candidates who accept public funds may spend no more than $50,000 from personal and immediate family funds.

10. A request for records under the Freedom of Information Act should be made by letter indicating as specifically as possible what is being sought. The requester should state that he or she is using the FOI Act. This letter should be sent to the Federal agency or agencies thought to possess the desired records. The lower left-hand corner of the envelope should be marked "FOIA Request." If a special form is needed to process your request, it will be sent by the agency. An access professional from the agency may telephone to clarify the request or discuss responsive materials. A requester may also appeal if the original request is denied.

BONUS. Following is a brief description of the usual stages by which a bill becomes law.

1. Introduction by a Member, who places it in the "hopper," a box on the Clerk's desk in the House Chamber; the bill is given a number and printed by the Government Printing Office so that copies are available the next morning.

2. Referral to one or more standing committees of the House by the Speaker, at the advice of the Parliamentarian.

3. Report from the committee or committees, after public hearings and "markup" meetings by subcommittee, committee, or both.

4. House approval of a special rule, reported by the House Rules Committee, making it in order for the House to consider the bill, and setting the terms for its debate and amendment.

5. Consideration of the bill in Committee of the Whole, in two stages: first, a time for general debate on the bill; and second, a time for amending the bill, one part at a time, under a rule that limits speeches on amendments to five minutes each.

6. Passage by the House after votes to confirm the amendments that were adopted in Committee of the Whole.

7. Transmittal to the Senate, by message.

8. Consideration and passage by the Senate—usually after referral to and reporting from a Senate committee—and after debate and amendment on the Senate floor.

9. Transmission from the Senate back to the House, with or without Senate amendments to the bill.

10. Resolution of differences between the House and the Senate, either through additional amendments between the Houses, or the report of a conference committee.

11. Enrollment on parchment paper and then signing by the Speaker and by the President of the Senate.

12. Transmittal to the President of the United States.

13. Approval or disapproval by the President; if the President disapproves, the bill will be returned with a veto message that explains reasons for the disapproval. A two-thirds vote in each chamber is needed to override a veto.

14. Filing with the Archivist of the United States as a new public law after approval of the President, or after passage by Congress overriding a veto.

Bills may be introduced in the Senate, and they follow essentially the same course of passage as bills first introduced and considered in the House of Representatives.

Quiz 13: A Legislative Glossary Quiz

1,s; 2,l; 3,p; 4,f; 5,i; 6,n; 7,y; 8,c; 9,q; 10,b; 11,g; 12,e; 13,d; 14,x; 15,j; 16,m; 17,a; 18,v; 19,r; 20,o; 21,w; 22,u; 23,h; 24,k; 25,t.

Note: *Because of the importance of the legislative terminology covered in this quiz, in addition to providing an Answer key, we are also including the terms and their definitions as text, to save having to go back to the quiz and match up the definition with the term.*

1. Act: Legislation which has passed both Houses of Congress, approved by the president, or passed over his veto, thus becoming law.

2. Advice and Consent: A process of Senate approval of executive and judicial appointments, and for treaties negotiated by the executive branch and signed by the President.

3. Bipartisanship: Cooperation between members of both political parties in either or both Houses, or between the President and Members of Congress representing the other party in addressing a particular issue or proposal.

4. Caucus: A meeting of Democratic Party members in the House, which elects party leaders and makes decisions on legislative business.

5. Cloture: A parliamentary device used in the Senate by which debate on a particular measure can be limited.

6. Confirmation: Action by the Senate, approving Presidential nominees for the executive branch, regulatory commissions, and certain other positions.

7. Contempt of Congress: Willful obstruction of the legislative process.

8. Continuing Resolution: A joint appropriations measure providing emergency funding for agencies whose regular appropriations bill has not been passed.

9. Filibuster: Debate typically characterized by individual Senators or groups of Senators speaking at extended length against a pending measure, often with the objective of frustrating action on the pending legislative proposals.

10. Germaneness: A House rule that amendments to a bill must relate to the subject matter under consideration.

11. Hearing: A meeting or session of a committee of Congress—usually open to the public—to obtain information and opinions on proposed legislation, to conduct an investigation, or oversee a program.

12. Joint Meeting: A meeting of both Houses of Congress, in which each Chamber recesses to meet for an occasion or ceremony, usually in the House Chamber.

13. Joint Session: A meeting of both Houses of Congress, customarily held in the House Chamber, held for necessary administrative and official purposes, e.g., the purpose of counting electoral votes, attending inaugurations, and to hear Presidential State of the Union messages.

14. Markup: The process in which congressional committees and subcommittees amend and rewrite proposed legislation in order to prepare it for consideration on the floor.

15. Memorial: A petition to Congress from State legislatures, usually requesting some sort of legislation, or expressing the sense of the State legislature on a particular question.

16. Petition: A request or plea sent to one or both Houses from an organization or private citizens' group asking support of particular legislation or favorable consideration of a matter.

17. Political Action Committee (PAC): A group organized to promote its members' views on selected issues, usually through raising money that is contributed to the campaign funds of candidates who support the group's position.

18. Quorum: The number of Members in each House necessary to conduct business.

19. Ratification: Either the act of approval of a proposed constitutional amendment by the legislatures of the States, or the Senate process of advice and consent to treaties negotiated by the President.

20. Rider: An unrelated amendment attached to a pending bill in order to improve its chances for passage.

21. Session: The period during which Congress assembles and carries on its regular business.

22. *Sine Die:* The final adjournment used to conclude a session of Congress.

23. Tabling Motion: A motion to stop action on a pending proposal and to lay it aside indefinitely.

24. Unanimous Consent: A practice in the House and Senate to set aside a rule of procedure, so as to expedite proceedings.

25. Veto: The constitutional procedure by which the President refuses to approve a bill or joint resolution and thus prevents its enactment into law.

Quiz 14: How Well Do You Know Washington, D.C.?

1. True.

2. f.

3. False. The Capitol Reflecting Pool is in front of the Grant Memorial.

4. b.

5. a.

6. True. When the Court is in session from October to June, the gallery is open to the public, although there are only 150 seats, available on a first-come, first-served basis.

7. d.

8. True.

9. c.

10. d.

Quiz 15: The Branches of the U.S.Military

1. Army: Five-Star General of the Army.

   Navy: Five-Star Fleet Admiral.

   Air Force: Four-Star General.

   Marine Corps: Four-Star General.

2. Army: Private Recruit.

   Navy: Seaman Recruit.

   Air Force: Airman Basic.

   Marine Corps: Private.

3. 1,d; 2,a; 3,e; 4,c; 5,b. (Source: *The Oxford Companion to American Military History*, p. 849, table titled "U.S. Military Service and Casualties in Major Wars and Conflicts, 1775–1991.")

4. b.

5. MREs are "Meals Ready to Eat"—individual, portable meals for military personnel in the field.

6. b.

7. True.

8. True. (The Commandant of the Marines is, however, a member of the Joint Chiefs of Staff.)

9. a.

10. c.

Quiz 16: Military Milestones

1,j; 2,a; 3,i; 4,n; 5,h; 6,c; 7,g; 8,m; 9,l; 10,d; 11,o; 12,e; 13,b; 14,k; 15,f.

Quiz 17: The Price of Freedom: American Battle Deaths in Twelve Wars

1,g; 2,f; 3,e; 4,k; 5,c; 6,b; 7,d; 8,j; 9,l; 10,h; 11,i; 12,a.[2]

Quiz 18: The Revolutionary War

1. b.

2. d.

3. b.

4. *Common Sense.*

5. Thomas Paine, in *Common Sense.*

6. True. In June 1778, "Headquarters Secret Service" was officially established.

7. c.

8. c.

9. a.

10. The Treaty of Paris.

Quiz 19: American Revolution Battles

1,g; 2,j; 3,a; 4,d; 5,b; 6,i; 7,c; 8,f; 9,e; 10,h.[3]

Quiz 20: An American Revolution Timeline Quiz

1,f; 2,o; 3,a; 4,k; 5,c; 6,m; 7,j; 8,b; 9,n; 10,h; 11,g; 12,l; 13,e; 14,i; 15,d.

Quiz 21: The War of 1812

1. a.

2. c.

3. c.

4. d.

5. False. The U.S. did attack Canada during the war, but they were defeated.

6. c.

7. b.

8. "We have met the enemy, and they are ours!" This was the message sent by naval commander Oliver Perry (see question #7) after he defeated the British during a battle on Lake Erie.

9. a. Jackson would go on to become the seventh President of the United States.

10. True. The Battle of New Orleans was fought two weeks after the peace treaty had been signed. At the time of the battle, the armies had not yet been informed of the cessation of hostilities.

Quiz 22: The Mexican War

1. b.

2. True.

3. The prevailing 1840s belief that the U.S. was destined (divinely, some said) to expand across the continent all the way to the Pacific Ocean. This was one of the reasons why the U.S. annexed Texas, which led to the Mexican War.

4. d.

5. a.

6. a.

7. b.

8. True. This incident was the inspiration for his seminal essay, *Civil Disobedience.*

9. True. Many U.S. soldiers of the time were recent immigrants who had hoped to improve their lot in life by coming to America. Many of these conscripts deserted rather than fight.

10. True.

BRAINBUSTER: c.

Quiz 23: The Civil War

1. b.

2. False.

3. False.

4. a, b.

5. c, on December 20, 1860.

6. True.

7. True.

8. Confederate. South Carolina militiamen fired on Fort Sumter when the commander of the fort refused to surrender.

9. General William Tecumseh Sherman.

10. d.

Quiz 24: Memorable Civil War Battles

1,c; 2,d; 3,a; 4,e; 5,g; 6,i; 7,f; 8,h; 9,b; 10,j.[4]

Quiz 25: Civil War Firsts

1,j; 2,f; 3,a; 4,b; 5,k; 6,i; 7,d; 8,l; 9,m; 10,c; 11,o; 12,n; 13,h; 14,e; 15,g.

Quiz 26: The Spanish-American War

1. c.

2. False. The Rough Riders were a volunteer cavalry group.

3. d.

4. b.

5. c.

6. False. "In 1975, [an] inquiry, headed by Adm. Hyman Rickover, reassessed the 1911 photographs of the wreckage, and concluded that the *Maine* was the victim of an internal explosion from spontaneous combustion in an inadequately vented bituminous coal bunker, which then exploded adjoining magazines."[5]

7. a.
8. The Treaty of Paris
9. d.
10. c.

Quiz 27: World War I

1. c.
2. a,b,d.
3. b.
4. True.
5. d.
6. d.
7. a.
8. a. The "b" answer is the number of Americans who served during World War II; the "c" answer, the number who served in the Vietnam War; the "d" answer, the number who served in the Persian Gulf War.[6]
9. "He kept us out of the war."
10. d.

Quiz 28: World War II

1. a,b,c.
2. e.
3. False. World War II began for the *United States* when the Japanese bombed Pearl Harbor, but WWII actually began in 1939 when Nazi Germany invaded Poland.
4. Winston Churchill.
5. False. The Battle of the Bulge was the *last* major offensive by the German army during World War II.
6. False. "V-J Day" marked the day the Allies were victorious over Japan during World War II. "V-E Day" marked the day the Allies were victorious in Europe during World War II.
7. True. The U.S. had to drop a second bomb on Nagasaki before the Japanese surrendered.
8. "Yesterday, December 7, 1941—a date which will live in infamy—the United States of America was suddenly and deliberately attacked by naval and air forces of the Empire of Japan."

9. b.

10. d.[7]

Quiz 29: The Korean War

1. d.

2. d.

3. True.

4. False. The majority of the United Nations troops that fought in the Korean War were American; 5,720,000 U.S. troops served in Korea.[8] A total of fifty-three UN member nations promised troops to assist South Korea, and, by the end of the war, twenty-two nations had sent just under 20,000 troops to Korea (less than one-half of 1 percent of the total "United Nations" deployment).[9]

5. b,d.

6. They were all powerful offensives by the Eighth Army against North Korea in 1951.

7. d.[10]

8. c.

9. True.

10. a.

Quiz 30: The Vietnam War

1. b.

2. False. Two-thirds of the men who served in Vietnam were volunteers. Two-thirds of the men who served in World War II were drafted.[11] Approximately 70 percent of those killed were volunteers.[12]

3. True. The last American troops departed Vietnam in their entirety on March 29, 1973. The United States fought to an agreed stalemate. The peace settlement was signed in Paris on January 27, 1973. It called for release of all U.S. prisoners, withdrawal of U.S. forces, limitation of both sides' forces inside South Vietnam and a commitment to peaceful reunification.[13]

4. False. No American had involvement in this incident near Trang Bang that burned Phan Thi Kim Phuc. The planes doing the bombing near the village were VNAF (Vietnam Air Force) and were being flown by Vietnamese pilots in support of South Vietnamese troops on the ground. The Vietnamese pilot who dropped the napalm in error is currently living in the United States. The incident in the photo took place on the second day of a three day battle between the North Vietnamese Army (NVA) who occu-

pied the village of Trang Bang, and the ARVN (Army of the Republic of Vietnam), who were trying to force the NVA out of the village. Recent reports in the news media that an American commander ordered the air strike that burned Kim Phuc are incorrect. There were no Americans involved in any capacity. "We [Americans] had nothing to do with controlling VNAF," according to Lieutenant General (Ret) James F. Hollingsworth, the Commanding General of TRAC at that time. Also, it has been incorrectly reported that two of Kim Phuc's brothers were killed in this incident. They were Kim's cousins not her brothers. [14]

5. a.

6. b.

7. Dwight D. Eisenhower, John F. Kennedy, Lyndon Johnson, and Richard Nixon.

8. c.

9. c.

10. d.[15]

Quiz 31: The Persian Gulf War

1. b.

2. True.

3. c.

4. False. The United Nations voted immediately to impose economic sanctions on Iraq.

5. d.

6. True.

7. 532,000.

8. a.

9. True.

10. b.

Quiz 32: The President's House

1. True.

2. True, except that Jefferson submitted his drawing anonymously, using only the initials "A.Z." Jefferson based his design on the Italian Rennaissance architect Palladio's Villa Rotonda.

3. A fortuitous thunderstorm. The walls of the White House today are the original walls.

4. False. The Oval Office is in the West Wing.

5. Benjamin Harrison.

6. William Howard Taft.

7. True.

8. d.

9. True.

10. There are **132** rooms, **35** bathrooms, and **6** levels in the Residence. There are also **412** doors, **147** windows, **28** fireplaces, **8** staircases, and **3** elevators. The White House kitchen has **5** full-time chefs. The kitchen can serve as many as **140** guests and hors d'oeuvres to more than **1,000** people.

Quiz 33: American Inventors and Inventions

1, t; 2, m; 3, z; 4, ww; 5, l; 6, a; 7, tt; 8, y; 9, pp; 10, b; 11, x; 12, w; 13, c; 14, ss; 15, dd; 16, ll; 17, e; 18, xx; 19, d; 20, mm; 21, r; 22, f; 23, n; 24, vv; 25, aa; 26, k; 27, o; 28, bb; 29, p; 30, kk; 31, ii; 32, g; 33, h; 34, qq; 35, i; 36, uu; 37, ff; 38, oo; 39, q; 40, rr; 41, ee; 42, j; 43, gg; 44, s; 45, nn; 46, v; 47, jj; 48, u; 49, cc; 50, hh.

Quiz 34: American Medical Breakthroughs

1. free dispensary 2. Benjamin Franklin 3. hemophilia 4. Dorothea Dix 5. ether 6. Philadelphia 7. New York 8. tuberculosis 9. sickle cell 10. cortisone 11. virology 12. estrogen 13. pacemaker 14. hereditary 15. heparin 16. fluoride 17. 1953 18. birth-control 19. angioplasty 20. t-Pa

Quiz 35: American Scientific Milestones

1. conveyor 2. cotton 3. Eli Whitney 4. Philadelphia 5. sewing 6. God wrought 7. weather 8. elevator 9. lock 10. telephone[16] 11. phonograph 12. light bulb 13. comet 14. Ford 15. cell 16. assembly 17. deep-freezing 18. expanding 19. earthquakes 20. one hundred 21. Harvard 22. carbon 23. supersonic 24. Idaho 25. bar code

Quiz 36: American Religious Milestones

1,g; 2,a; 3,j; 4,b; 5,i; 6,c; 7,d; 8,e; 9,f; 10,h.

Quiz 37: The History of the U.S. Space Program

1. a.

2. March 1926, in an orchard in Auburn, Massachusetts.

3. c.

4. b.

5. False. The Russian satellite *Sputnik* was launched into orbit around the earth in October, 1957.

6. c.

7. Skylab.

8. The sixteen nations are the United States, Canada, Brazil, Russia, Belgium, France, Germany, Netherlands, Japan, United Kingdom, Switzerland, Sweden, Spain, Italy, Norway, and Denmark.

9. d.

10. One small step for man, one giant leap for mankind.[17]

Quiz 38: The Apollo Moon Missions

1,h; 2,b; 3,e; 4,a; 5,i; 6,g; 7,d; 8,f; 9,c.

Quiz 39: The Apollo Code Names Quiz

1,h; 2,a; 3,e; 4,i; 5,g; 6,b; 7,f; 8,d; 9,c.

Quiz 40: The Space Shuttle

1. d.

2. False. The Space Shuttle main engine delivers as much horsepower as *thirty-nine* locomotives.

3. d.

4. 7.3 million.

5. a.

6. d.

7. True.

8. c.

9. d.

10. True.

Quiz 41: The Space Station

1. True. It has forty-three thousand cubic feet of living and working space for astronauts.

2. b.

3. c.

4. Less. There is less effort expended in a microgravity environment so less sleep is required for restoration.

5. True.

6. d.

7. b.

8. d.

9. The United States, Russia, Canada, Japan, Belgium, Brazil, Denmark, France, Germany, Italy, the Netherlands, Norway, Spain, Sweden, Switzerland, and the United Kingdom.

10. True.

Quiz 42: American Actors

1. False. He was the only juror to vote "Not Guilty."

2. Jack Nicholson.

3. d.

4. Paul Newman.

5. False. It was Dustin Hoffman.

6. 1,d; 2,c; 3,a; 4,b; 5,e.

7. James Cagney, starring as George M. Cohan in 1942's *Yankee Doodle Dandy*.

8. Marlon Brando.

9. False. The role was played by William Holden.

10. David Niven.

Quiz 43: American Art and Artists

1,h; 2,a; 3,e; 4,j; 5,d; 6,b; 7,c; 8,g; 9,f; 10,i.

Quiz 44: American Best-Sellers of the Past Fifty Years

1. *Kon-Tiki.*

2. *The Catcher in the Rye* by J.D. Salinger.

3. *East of Eden.*

4. Alfred Kinsey.

5. Positive thinking.

6. *Peyton Place* by Grace Metalious.

7. *The Search for Bridey Murphy* by Morey Bernstein.

8. *Lolita* by Vladimir Nabokov.

9. *Lady Chatterley's Lover.*

10. *The Rise and Fall of the Third Reich.*

11. *Tropic of Cancer.* The second volume was *Black Spring* (1936); the third volume, *Tropic of Capricorn* (1939).

12. *Sex and the Single Girl.*

13. *In His Own Write* by John Lennon.

14. *Valley of the Dolls.*

15. *In Cold Blood.*

16. *Rosemary's Baby.*

17. *The Godfather* by Mario Puzo, a 1969 best-seller.

18. *Love Story* by Erich Segal, a 1970 best-seller.

19. *Everything You Always Wanted to Know About Sex but Were Afraid to Ask* by David Reuben, M.D.

20. *The Exorcist* by William Peter Blatty, a 1971 best-seller.

21. *Seagull.*

22. *Jaws,* by Peter Benchley, a 1974 best-seller.

23. *All the President's Men* by Carl Bernstein and Bob Woodward, a 1974 non-fiction best-seller.

24. *The Silmarillion* by J.R.R. Tolkien.

25. *Roots* by Alex Haley, a 1977 best-seller.

26. *Mommie Dearest.*

27. 1979's *The Dead Zone.*

28. *The Complete Scarsdale Medical Diet* by Dr. Herman Tarnower.

29. *When Bad Things Happen to Good People,* by Harold S. Kushner, a 1982 best-seller.

30. *The G Spot and Other Recent Discoveries about Human Sexuality* by Alice Kahn Ladas.

31. *His Way: The Unauthorized Biography of Frank Sinatra.*

32. *A Brief History of Time: From the Big Bang to Black Holes.*

33. *The Satanic Verses.*

34. 1991's *Scarlett,* by Alexander Ripley.

35. 1992's *The Way Things Ought To Be.*

36. 1992's *Sex.*

37. 1993's *Private Parts.*

38. John Gray's 1993 best-seller, *Men Are from Mars, Women Are from Venus.*

39. *Primary Colors,* later revealed to be by Joe Klein.

40. 1997's *Harry Potter and the Sorcerer's Stone* by J.K. Rowlings.

Quiz 45: American Movies

1. *Gone With the Wind* (1939).
2. *The Godfather* (1972).
3. *Taxi Driver* (1976).
4. *The Wizard of Oz* (1939).
5. *Double Indemnity* (1944).
6. *Psycho* (1960).
7. *E.T. The Extra-Terrestrial* (1982).
8. *Citizen Kane* (1941).
9. *The Silence of the Lambs* (1991).
10. *Animal House* (1978).
11. *Annie Hall* (1977).
12. *GoodFellas* (1990).
13. *Rocky* (1976).
14. *A Clockwork Orange* (1971).
15. *2001: A Space Odyssey* (1968).

Quiz 46: American Music

1. True. The music of the American Indian was mostly chanting and singing on a five-note scale.
2. True.
3. c.
4. b.
5. a.
6. *Paris*
7. True.
8. Leonard Bernstein.
9. *Spring*.
10. Glass, Einstein.

Quiz 47: American Sports

1. a.
2. Ripken took a day off, thus ending his string of 2,632 consecutive games started. Ripken had earlier broken the record of 2,130 consecutive games held by "The Iron Horse," the Yankees' Lou Gehrig—a record which had stood since 1939.
3. The Super Bowl was dreamed up by the NFL's first commissioner, Pete Rozelle, and the first Super Bowl was played January 15, 1967 (The Green Bay Packers beat the Kansas City Chiefs by the score of 35–10).
4. The golf phenom entered the pro golf circuit in 1996, still shy of his twenty-first birthday.
5. a,2 (#3); b,3 (#24); c,4 (#43); d,1 (#6).
6. c.
7. The Red Sox played their first game in Fenway Park on April 20, 1912. Wrigley Field opened four years later.

8. False: While Bush did not do a flyover or even land a jet anywhere near the stadium, he did throw out the first pitch at the World Series—no mean feat considering the game was played in New York City only weeks after the September 11 attacks, and America was on the brink of war.

9. In 1973, OJ Simpson of the Buffalo Bills rushed for 2,003 yards, the most in a season. In 1984, second-year back Eric Dickerson broke the record, rushing for 2,105 yards for the Los Angeles Rams.

10. b.

11. b.

12. a. Spitz won seven gold medals in the 1972 Olympics in Munich.

13. Six.

14. In his twenty-two-year pitching career (from 1890 to 1911), he had 511 wins, the all-time leader. Every year, in his honor, baseball presents the Cy Young Award to a pitcher in the National and American leagues in recognition of their accomplishments.

15. b. The Rams moved from Los Angeles to St. Louis in 1995.

16. False. Wilt Chamberlain, center for the Philadelphia Warriors, scored 100 points on March 2, 1962. Needless to say Philadelphia beat the New York Knicks by a score of 169 to 147.

17. The Orlando Magic, who drafted Shaq after his junior year at Louisiana State Univerity.

18. The space the length of a ball between the two scrimmage lines. The offensive team and defensive team must remain behind their end of the ball.

19. "<u>Today</u>, I consider <u>myself</u> the <u>luckiest</u> man on the face of the <u>earth</u>." This was part of Lou Gehrig's farewell speech given at Yankee Stadium on July 4, 1939. Gehrig was forced to retire after being stricken by Amyotrophic Lateral Sclerosis. He had played his last game on May 2, 1939, after starting a record 2,130 consecutive games.

20. Joe Dimaggio of the Yankees set the record in 1941 by hitting safely in fifty-six consecutive games. We'd say it's a record that will probably never be broken, but we've learned never to say never in baseball!

Quiz 48: American TV

1. b.

2. c.

3. False. The longest running Western on network TV was *Gunsmoke*, which ran on CBS from 1955 through 1975.

4. Fred and Ethel.

5. d.

6. John Ross.

7. There is nothing wrong with your <u>television set</u>. Do not attempt to adjust the <u>picture</u>. We are controlling <u>transmission</u>. We will control the <u>horizontal</u>. We will control the <u>vertical</u>. We can change the focus to a <u>soft</u> blur—or sharpen it to <u>crystal</u> clarity. For the next <u>hour</u>, sit quietly and we will <u>control</u> all that you <u>see</u> and <u>hear</u>. You are about to <u>participate</u> in a great <u>adventure</u>. You are about to experience the awe and <u>mystery</u> which reaches from the inner <u>mind</u> to . . . the *Outer Limits*.

8. a.

9. False. It meant, "Live long and prosper."

10. f.

Quiz 49: American Writers and Poets

1,m; 2,bb; 3,ddd; 4,a; 5,uuu; 6,h; 7,v; 8,jj; 9,d; 10,aaa; 11,www;
12,dd; 13,ss; 14,aa; 15,ww; 16,rrr; 17,z; 18,gg; 19,x; 20,mm; 21,tt;
22,e; 23,vvv; 24,q; 25,b; 26,y; 27,i; 28,k; 29,rr; 30,zz; 31,cc; 32,jjj;
33,sss; 34,f; 35,ll; 36,ppp; 37,uu; 38,g; 39,pp; 40,j; 41,qq; 42,mmm;
43,iii; 44,oo; 45,ttt; 46,xx; 47,kkk; 48,vv; 49,n; 50,c; 51,qqq; 52,u;
53,ee; 54,bbb; 55,ff; 56,ooo; 57,l; 58,p; 59,hh; 60,r; 61,lll; 62,t;
63,eee; 64,o; 65,fff; 66,nnn; 67,yy; 68,ggg; 69,w; 70,hhh; 71,ccc;
72,s; 73,wwww; 74,dddd; 75,rrrr; 76,zzz; 77,ssss; 78,llll; 79,uuuu;
80,mmmm; 81,gggg; 82,xxx; 83,iiii; 84,ii; 85,kk; 86,aaaa; 87,ffff;
88,tttt; 89,pppp; 90,kkkk; 91,yyy; 92,jjjj; 93,nn; 94,oooo; 95,vvvv;
96,qqqq; 97,nnnn; 98,cccc; 99,bbbb; 100,eeee; 101,hhhh.

Quiz 50: Independence Day

1. True.

2. b.

3. Thirteen.

4. False. The document was not completely signed until early August 1776.

5. c.

6. So "King George can read that without spectacles!"

7. a.

8. True.

9. The Liberty Bell.

10. d.

Quiz 51: Memorial Day

1. b.

2. a.

3. True.

4. c.

5. d.

6. False. By 1890, it was only observed by the Northern states.

7. True.

8. True.

9. d.

10. True. On January 19, 1999, Senator Inouye of Hawaii introduced bill S. 189 to the Senate. This bill proposes to restore the observance of Memorial Day back to May 30th instead of "the last Monday in May." On April 19, 1999, Representative Gibbons introduced the bill to the House (H.R. 1474). The bills were referred to the Committee on the Judiciary and the Committee on Government Reform. Nothing has happened with these bills of late.

Quiz 52: Labor Day

1. Samuel Gompers, founder and longtime president of the American Federation of Labor.

2. a.

3. True.

4. c.

5. d.

6. b.

7. a.

8. True.

9. d.

10. Labor Sunday.

Quiz 53: Thanksgiving

1. c.

2. True.

3. d.

4. a.

5. b.

6. d.

7. True. Three Indian chiefs and ninety Indians ate with the Pilgrims in 1621.

8. False. Thanksgiving celebrations of the 1700s were days of fasting and prayer.

9. c.

10. a.

Quiz 54: The Articles of Confederation

1. True.

2. Thirteen.

3. New Hampshire, Massachusetts, Rhode Island, Connecticut, New York, New Jersey, Pennsylvania, Delaware, Maryland, Virginia, North Carolina, South Carolina, and Georgia.

4. d.

5. c.

6. a.

7. False. There was no provision for a President in the Articles of Confederation. The office of the President was created in Article II, Section 1 of the United States Constitution.

8. False. The Articles of Confederation did not permit the government to collect taxes.

9. d.

10. The United States Constitution, which went into effect in 1789.

Quiz 55: The Declaration of Independence

1. When in the <u>course</u> of <u>human</u> events, it becomes necessary for one <u>people</u> to <u>dissolve</u> the political <u>bands</u> which have <u>connected</u> them with <u>another</u>, and to assume among the <u>powers</u> of the <u>earth</u>, the <u>separate</u> and <u>equal</u> station to which the <u>laws</u> of <u>nature</u> and of nature's <u>God</u> entitle them, a <u>decent</u> respect to the <u>opinions</u> of <u>mankind</u> requires that they should <u>declare</u> the <u>causes</u> which impel them to the <u>separation</u>.

2. a,b,d.

3. True. "He has erected a multitude of new offices, and sent hither swarms of officers to harass our people and eat out their substance."

4. True. "He has affected to render the military independent of, and superior to, the civil power."

5. Fifty-six. The following list is from the author's *The U.S.A. Book of Lists* and is reprinted with permission.

THE SIGNERS OF THE DECLARATION OF INDEPENDENCE
AND THEIR OCCUPATIONS

(NOTE: There were only fifty-six signers of the Declaration of Independence, but the total men listed here number sixty-three, because some of the Founders had two or more occupations. They are so listed individually.)

Judge (15)

Josiah Bartlett (NH); Samuel Chase (MD); Stephen Hopkins (RI); Frances Hopkinson (NJ); Samuel Huntington (CT); John Morton (PA); William Paca (MD); Robert Treat Paine (MA); George Read (DE); Caesar Rodney (DE); George Ross (PA); George Walton (GA); William Whipple (NH); James Wilson (PA); Oliver Wolcott (CT).

Lawyer (14)

John Adams (MA); Charles Carroll (MD); William Ellery (RI); Thomas Heyward, Jr. (SC); William Hooper (NC); Thomas Jefferson (VA); Thomas McKean (DE); John Penn (NC); Edward Rutledge (SC); Roger Sherman (CT); James Smith (PA); Richard Stockton (NJ); Thomas Stone (MD); George Wythe (VA).

Farmer (10)

Carter Braxton (VA); Benjamin Harrison (VA); John Hart (NJ); Thomas Heyward, Jr. (SC); Francis Lightfoot Lee (VA); Henry Richard Lee (VA); Thomas Lynch, Jr. (SC); Arthur Middleton (SC); Lewis Morris (NY); Thomas Nelson, Jr. (VA).

Merchant (10)

George Clymer (PA); Elbridge Gerry (MA); Button Gwinnett (GA); John Hancock (MA); Joseph Hewes (NC); Francis Lewis (NY); Philip Livingston (NY); Robert Morris (PA); William Whipple (NH); William Williams (CT).

Physician (4)

Josiah Bartlett (NH); Lyman Hall (GA); Benjamin Rush (PA); Matthew Thornton (NH).

Educator (2)

Stephen Hopkins (RI); John Witherspoon (NJ).

Author (1)

Frances Hopkinson (NJ).

Clergyman (1)

John Witherspoon (NJ).

Ironmaster (1)

George Taylor (PA).

Political Leader (1)
    Samuel Adams (MA).

Printer (1)
    Benjamin Franklin (PA).

Publisher (1)
    Benjamin Franklin (PA).

Surveyor (1)
    Abraham Clark (NJ).

Soldier (1)
    William Floyd (NY).

6. Fifteen Judges signed the Declaration of Independence.
7. July 4, 1776.
8. Thomas Jefferson. It was edited and revised by John Adams and Benjamin Franklin.
9. Natural law.
10. The southern colonies objected to it, asserting that it was a slur against the institution of slavery.

Quiz 56: The Constitution

1. We the <u>People</u> of the United States, in Order to form a more perfect <u>Union</u>, establish <u>Justice</u>, insure domestic <u>Tranquility</u>, provide for the common <u>defense</u>, promote the general <u>Welfare</u>, and secure the <u>Blessings</u> of Liberty to ourselves and our <u>Posterity</u>, do <u>ordain</u> and <u>establish</u> this <u>Constitution</u> for the United States of America.
2. The Congress of the United States.
3. Twenty-five.
4. Two.
5. Thirty.
6. True. Article I, Section 8 of the Constitution states, "The Congress shall have Power To lay and collect Taxes, Duties, Imposts and Excises, to pay the Debts and provide for the common Defence and general Welfare of the United States . . ."
7. False. The President cannot declare war. That power is granted only to Congress in Article I, Section 8 of the Constitution. (Interestingly, this has

long been interpreted to mean that the President can *wage* war by ordering troops into combat as Commander in Chief of the U.S. Armed Forces, a power granted him in Article II, Section 2, but that an official *declaration* of war must come from the Congress.)

8. False. Article I, Section 10 states that "No State shall enter into any Treaty, Alliance, or Confederation; grant Letters of Marque and Reprisal; coin Money; emit Bills of Credit; make any Thing but gold and silver Coin a Tender in Payment of Debts; pass any Bill of Attainder, ex post facto Law, or Law impairing the Obligation of Contracts, or grant any Title of Nobility."

9. Article II, Section 1 of the Constitution states that in order to run for President, a person must be thirty-five years old, a native-born American citizen, and *must have been a resident of the United States for the previous fourteen years.*

10. There is no specific requirement in the Constitution as to how often the President must deliver a State of the Union address. Article II, Section 3 simply states that "he shall from time to time give to the Congress . . ." Presidents have traditionally interpreted "time to time" to mean annually.

11. Treason, bribery, and high Crimes and Misdemeanors. (Article II, Section 4.) Removal from office may only be carried out upon *conviction* of the charges levied.

12. False. Article III, Section 1 of the Constitution states that the Justices shall receive "a Compensation which shall not be diminished during their Continuance in Office."

13. Two. (Article III, Section 3.)

14. False. "[N]o new State shall be formed or erected within the Jurisdiction of any other State . . ." (Article IV, Section 3.)

15. True. He signed as "President and Deputy from Virginia."

Quiz 57: The Bill of Rights

Article I: Congress shall make no <u>law</u> respecting an establishment of <u>religion</u>, or prohibiting the free exercise thereof; or abridging the freedom of <u>speech</u>, or of the <u>press</u>; or of the right of the <u>people</u> peaceably to <u>assemble</u>, and to <u>petition</u> the <u>government</u> for a redress of <u>grievances</u>.

Article II: A well-regulated <u>militia</u>, being necessary to the <u>security</u> of a free <u>State</u>, the right of the people to keep and bear <u>arms</u>, shall not be <u>infringed</u>.

Article III: No <u>soldier</u> shall, in time of <u>peace</u> be quartered in any <u>house</u>, without the <u>consent</u> of the <u>owner</u>, nor in time of <u>war</u>, but in a <u>manner</u> prescribed by <u>law</u>.

Article IV: The <u>right</u> of the people to be <u>secure</u> in their <u>persons</u>, houses, <u>papers</u>, and effects, against unreasonable <u>search</u> and <u>seizures</u>, shall not be violated, and no <u>warrants</u> shall issue, but upon <u>probable cause</u>, supported by oath or <u>affirmation</u>, and particularly describing the <u>place</u> to be <u>searched</u>, and the <u>persons</u> or <u>things</u> to be <u>seized</u>.

Article V: No person shall be held to <u>answer</u> for a <u>capital</u>, or otherwise <u>infamous</u> crime, unless on a presentment or <u>indictment</u> of a <u>Grand Jury</u>, except in cases arising in the <u>land</u> or <u>naval</u> forces, or in the <u>militia</u>, when in actual <u>service</u> in time of <u>war</u> or <u>public danger</u>; nor shall any <u>person</u> be <u>subject</u> for the same <u>offense</u> to be <u>twice</u> put in <u>jeopardy</u> of life or <u>limb</u>; nor shall be compelled in any <u>criminal</u> case to be a witness against <u>himself</u>, nor be <u>deprived</u> of life, <u>liberty</u>, or property, without due <u>process</u> of law; nor shall <u>private</u> property be taken for <u>public</u> use, without just <u>compensation</u>.

Article VI: In all criminal <u>prosecutions</u>, the <u>accused</u> shall enjoy the right to a <u>speedy</u> and <u>public</u> trial, by an impartial <u>jury</u> of the State and district wherein the <u>crime</u> shall have been <u>committed</u>, which <u>district</u> shall have been previously ascertained by <u>law</u>, and to be <u>informed</u> of the <u>nature</u> and cause of the <u>accusation</u>; to be <u>confronted</u> with the <u>witnesses</u> against him; to have <u>compulsory</u> process for obtaining <u>witnesses</u> in his favor, and to have the assistance of <u>counsel</u> for his <u>defense</u>.

Article VII: In suits at <u>common</u> law, where the <u>value</u> in <u>controversy</u> shall exceed <u>twenty</u> dollars, the right of <u>trial</u> by <u>jury</u> shall be <u>preserved</u>, and no <u>fact</u> tried by a <u>jury</u>, shall be otherwise <u>reexamined</u> in any Court of the <u>United States</u>, than according to <u>rules</u> of common <u>law</u>.

Article VIII: Excessive <u>bail</u> shall not be required, nor excessive <u>fines</u> imposed, nor <u>cruel</u> and <u>unusual</u> punishments inflicted.

Article IX: The enumeration in the <u>Constitution</u>, of certain <u>rights</u>, shall not be construed to <u>deny</u> or <u>disparage</u> others retained by the <u>people</u>.

Article X: The <u>powers</u> not delegated to the <u>United</u> States by the <u>Constitution</u>, nor <u>prohibited</u> by it to the <u>States</u>, are reserved to the <u>States</u> respectively, or to the <u>people</u>.

Quiz 58: The Amendments

1. Mississippi.

2. Tennessee.

3. True.

4. It forbade the "manufacture, sale, or transportation of intoxicating liquors" in the United States, ushering in Prohibition.

5. Section 1 of the Twenty-first Amendment ended Prohibition.

6. True.

7. The Vice President-elect would be sworn in as President.

8. True. The amendment states: "No person shall be elected to the office of the President *more than twice . . .*" [emphasis added]. Bill Clinton was elected to the office of the President twice, and is therefore ineligible to run again. A Constitutional amendment would be required to modify or repeal the Twenty-second Amendment in order for him to be able to run.

9. Mississippi.

10. True.

Quiz 59: The Gettysburg Address

1. The dedication of a military cemetery at Gettysburg, Pennsylvania.

2. November 19, 1863.

3. Nation.

4. Five. The Library of Congress owns two. The other three copies of the Address were written by Lincoln for charitable purposes well after November 19. The copy for Edward Everett, the orator who spoke at Gettysburg for two hours prior to Lincoln, is at the Illinois State Historical Library at Springfield; the Bancroft copy, requested by historian George Bancroft, is at Cornell University; the Bliss copy was made for Colonel Alexander Bliss, Bancroft's stepson, and is now in the Lincoln Room of the White House. [18]

5. English, French, Portuguese, Spanish, Italian, German, Dutch, Danish, Norwegian-Bokmal, Swedish, Finnish, Polish, Czech, Slovak, Russian, Hungarian, Serbo-Croatian, Greek, Turkish, Persian, Arabic, Hebrew, Urdu, Hindi, Burmese, Chinese, Korean, Japanese, and Tagalog.

6. Four score and seven years equals eighty-seven years. Eighty-seven years before November 19, 1863, the date of the Gettysburg Address was the year 1776, the year of the Declaration of Independence.

7. "The world will little note, nor long remember, what we say here . . ."

8. False. According to the Library of Congress, one picture exists. It shows Lincoln seated and hatless, flanked on his right side by his bodyguard, and is believed to have been taken approximately two hours before he delivered the Address.

9. True. Lincoln's source for the quote was an 1850 sermon by Theodore Parker which contained the phrase, "a government of all the people, by all the people, for all the people."

10. David Mills of the Gettysburg Cemetery Commission.

Quiz 60: The Louisiana Purchase

1. a.

2. b.

3. Monroe, Robert.

4. c.

5. True, even though the French had no such intentions.

6. d.

7. False. The Louisiana Purchase doubled the size of the United States.

8. Meriwether Lewis and William Clark.

9. Arkansas, Colorado, Iowa, Kansas, Louisiana, Minnesota, Missouri, Montana, Nebraska, North Dakota, Oklahoma, South Dakota, and Wyoming.

10. b. The official transfer of the territory took place in New Orleans on December 20, 1803, but the Treaty authorizing the purchase was signed in Paris on May 2, 1803.

Quiz 61: The Monroe Doctrine

1. True. The "Monroe Doctrine" was first stated in President Monroe's seventh Annual Message to Congress.

2. c.

3. The Western hemisphere is no longer subject to European colonization.

4. a.

5. True.

6. True.

7. President Theodore Roosevelt, on December 6, 1904, 81 years after President Monroe stated the Monroe Doctrine.

8. d.

9. True.

10. True.[19]

Quiz 62: The American Flag: A Star-Spangled Quiz

1. b, Sweden (1495); c, Denmark (1219); e, The Netherlands (1643).

2. c.

3. a.

4. Francis Scott Key wrote the lyrics; the melody is an old English drinking song called, "To Ancreon in Heaven."

5. It was signed into law by President Herbert Hoover on March 3, 1931.

6. There are thirteen alternating red and white stripes on the flag.

7. The stripes symbolize the thirteen original colonies.

8. True.

9. "Although burning is the preferred method, it is also permissible simply to cut the flag into small pieces so it is no longer recognizable as a flag. Then, whether the remainder is ashes or pieces of cloth, it may be buried or simply sealed in a bag or box for trash collection. The latter is not disrespectful and, for those without access to a plot of land, may be the only viable means of disposal. Some veterans' posts scatter the ashes on land, at sea or from the air."[20]

10. False. A design for a flag with fifty-one stars already exists.

Quiz 63: Flag Protocol

1. False. When raising a flag to half-staff, it should be raised briskly to the *top* of the flagpole for a moment, and then lowered to the halfway point.

2. c.

3. b.

4. True.

5. 1,c; 2,a; 3,b.

6. a.

7. True.

8. False. There is *always* a flag displayed outside polling places on election days.

9. c. "The Stars and Stripes Forever," composed by John Philip Sousa in 1897, was designated our National March by Congress in 1987.

10. The only person who has ever been honored for cutting an American flag into pieces was explorer Robert Peary. Upon his arrival at the North Pole in 1909, Peary cut up a flag and left pieces scattered all over the area.

Quiz 64: The Ten Greatest American Speeches Quiz

1. Martin Luther King, Wednesday, August 28, 1963.

2. John F. Kennedy, Friday, January 20, 1961.

3. Franklin Delano Roosevelt, Saturday, March 4, 1933.

4. Franklin Delano Roosevelt, Monday, December 8, 1941.

5. Barbara Jordan, Monday, July 12, 1976.

6. Richard Nixon, Tuesday, September 23, 1952.

7. Malcolm X, April 13, 1964.

8. Ronald Reagan, Tuesday, January 28, 1986 (the day of the space shuttle *Challenger* explosion).

9. John F. Kennedy (then a Senator), Monday, September 12, 1960 (speech to the Greater Houston Ministerial Association).

10. Lyndon B. Johnson, Monday, March 15, 1965 (after the voting riots in Selma, Alabama).

Quiz 65: The First Ladies

1,l; 2,a; 3,cc; 4,n; 5,m; 6,nn; 7,s; 8,e; 9,ff; 10,q,t; 11,aa; 12,o; 13,gg,ii; 14,z; 15,bb; 16,pp; 17,ee; 18,b; 19,c; 20,r; 21,d; 22,f,v; 23,u; 24,w,hh; 25,x; 26,y,dd; 27,g; 28,k; 29,h; 30,p; 31,i; 32,j; 33,oo; 34,ll; 35,mm; 36,kk; 37,qq; 38,jj,ss; 39,tt; 40,rr.

Quiz 66: The Presidents' Children

1. John Quincy Adams.

2. Maria Hester Monroe.

3. John Scott Harrison was the son of William Henry Harrison and the father of Benjamin Harrison.

4. John Tyler, Jr.

5. Robert Todd Lincoln.

6. Jesse Root Grant.

7. Ruth Cleveland.

8. Theodore Roosevelt, Jr.

9. Amy Carter.

10. Barbara and Jenna Bush.

Quiz 67: American National Parks

1,q; 2,cc; 3,e; 4,a; 5,pp; 6,oo; 7,t; 8,ee; 9,nn; 10,z; 11,rr; 12,i; 13,r; 14,aa; 15,ee; 16,mm; 17,j; 18,m; 19,t; 20,h; 21,jj; 22,m; 23,q; 24,hh; 25,e; 26,f; 27,kk; 28,dd; 29,l; 30,kk; 31,gg; 32,gg; 33,e; 34,i; 35,gg; 36,hh; 37,h; 38,c; 39,h; 40,h; 41,s; 42,gg; 43,rr; 44,x; 45,kk; 46,a; 47,z; 48,e; 49,qq; 50,d; 51,ff; 52,oo; 53,pp; 54,x; 55,l; 56.gg; 57,c;

58,hh; 59,r; 60,x; 61,j; 62,s; 63,kk; 64,e; 65,a; 66,h; 67,e; 68,cc; 69,o;
70,n; 71,h; 72,z; 73,s; 74,s; 75,pp; 76,rr; 77,j; 78,gg; 79,f; 80,s; 81,nn;
82,d; 83,qq; 84,nn; 85,a; 86,h; 87,qq; 88,d; 89,p; 90,d; 91,x; 92,ee;
93,d; 94,v; 95,w; 96,qq; 97,k; 98,g; 99,d; 100,f; 101,ll; 102,u; 103,e;
104,b; 105,oo; 106,v; 107,gg; 108,p; 109,h; 110,gg; 111,rr; 112,bb;
113,h; 114,t; 115,ee; 116,y; 117,b; 118,k; 119,x; 120,y; 121,h; 122,h;
123,ii; 124,ee; 125,hh; 126,gg; 127,aa; 128,e.

Quiz 68: Which American Said It?

1,j; 2,a; 3,l; 4,b; 5,f; 6,s; 7,c; 8,d; 9,m; 10,g; 11,t; 12,i; 13,r; 14,k;
15,q; 16,n; 17,y; 18,p; 19,w; 20,x; 21,u; 22,o; 23,e; 24,v; 25,h.

Quiz 69: American National Monuments

1. b.
2. False. The Korean War Veterans Memorial is located in Washington, D.C.
3. a.
4. b, on the South Wall; d, on the North Wall.
5. False. No federal funds were used for the construction of the Vietnam Veterans Memorial. Close to $9 million in private funds were raised for the Memorial.
6. d.
7. False. The bodies of many of the 1,177 crewmen killed during the attack on Pearl Harbor remain in the *Arizona*, honorably buried at sea.
8. g.
9. False. The Statue was a gift from France.
10. c.

Quiz 70: American Food

1. Cracker Jack
2. Tomato
3. Sanka
4. Moon Pie
5. White Castle
6. Green Giant
7. 7-Up
8. Lay's Potato Chips
9. Trix cereal
10. Tang
11. McDonald's Big Mac
12. Eggo (Waffles)
13. Reeses Pieces
14. Spam
15. Alka-Seltzer

Quiz 71: American Tourist Attractions

1,a; 2,b; 3,c; 4,d; 5,e; 6,f; 7,g; 8,h; 9,i; 10,j; 11,k; 12,l; 13,m; 14,n; 15,o; 16,p; 17,q; 18,r; 19,s; 20,t; 21,u; 22,v; 23,w; 24,x; 25,y; 26,z; 27,aa; 28,bb; 29,cc; 30,dd; 31,ee. (*These places are so strange, we did not have it in our heart to place them anywhere other than where they belong!*)

Quiz 72: American Geography

1. Utah, Colorado, Arizona, and New Mexico.

2. Michigan and Wisconsin.

3. Delaware.

4. California.

5. They all have a coastline: Hawaii (Pacific Ocean), Oregon (Pacific Ocean), Texas (Gulf of Mexico), Georgia (Atlantic Ocean), Virginia (Atlantic Ocean), New Jersey (Atlantic Ocean), Indiana (Lake Michigan), Maine (Atlantic Ocean), Pennsylvania (Lake Erie), Minnesota (Lake Superior).

6. True. According to the United States Census Bureau, Wyoming's population as of July 1, 1999, was 479,602.

7. True.

8. It's in both. The line of demarcation runs through the northwest corner of Florida, placing some counties of the state in the Central Time Zone.

9. The thirteen original states and the date of their admission to the Union are: 1. Delaware (Friday, December 7, 1787); 2. Pennsylvania (Wednesday, December 12, 1787); 3. New Jersey (Tuesday, December 18, 1787); 4. Georgia (Friday, January 2, 1788); 5. Connecticut (Friday, January 9, 1788); 6. Massachusetts (Friday, February 6, 1788); 7. Maryland (Wednesday, April 28, 1788); 8. South Carolina (Sunday, May 23, 1788); 9. New Hampshire (Monday, June 21, 1788); 10. Virginia (Friday, June 25, 1788); 11. New York (Monday, July 26, 1788); 12. North Carolina (Saturday, November 21, 1789); 13. Rhode Island (Saturday, May 29, 1790).

10. Alaska, which was admitted as the forty-ninth state in 1959. The territory of Alaska was purchased from Russia in 1867 for $7,200,000 in a deal negotiated by then-Secretary of State William H. Seward. The insulting epithet was dropped after gold was discovered in the state in the late 1800s.

Quiz 73: State Motto Quiz

1,j; 2,a; 3,l; 4,v; 5,p; 6,m; 7,hh; 8,g; 9,cc; 10,ff; 11,ww; 12,b; 13,y; 14,e; 15,z; 16,c; 17,qq; 18,r; 19,ss; 20,f; 21,ii; 22,s; 23,aa; 24,d; 25,xx;

26,t; 27,d; 28,i; 29,kk; 30,w; 31,u; 32,x; 33,h; 34,bb; 35,jj; 36,n; 37,vv; 38,o; 39,uu; 40,ll; 41,q; 42,tt; 43,mm; 44,ee; 45,nn; 46,oo; 47,k; 48,pp; 49,rr; 50,gg; 51,yy.

Quiz 74: State Capitals Quiz

1,ff; 2,aa; 3,kk; 4,dd; 5,pp; 6,p; 7,u; 8,r; 9,vv; 10,c; 11,w; 12,h; 13,tt; 14,x; 15,q; 16,ww; 17,s; 18,f; 19,d; 20,b; 21,i; 22,bb; 23,uu; 24,y; 25,z; 26,v; 27,cc; 28,j; 29,o; 30,xx; 31,ss; 32,a; 33,nn; 34,g; 35,n; 36,ii; 37,qq; 38,t; 39,mm; 40,m; 41,ll; 42,hh; 43,e; 44,rr; 45,gg; 46,oo; 47,jj; 48,k; 49,ee; 50,l.

Quiz 75: American Fads and Crazes

1. The Cakewalk.
2. The Daisy Air Rifle (it shot BBs).
3. d.
4. The Tango.
5. *Gone With the Wind.*
6. Rosie the Riveter.
7. The Hula Hoop.
8. The Twist.
9. Streaking.
10. Michelangelo, Leonardo, Donatello, and Raphael—the Teenage Mutant Ninja Turtles.

Quiz 76: The Library of Congress

1. b.
2. b.
3. False. Thousands of visitors, scholars, researchers, and others from all over the world visit the Library of Congress each year.
4. True.
5. d.
6. d. (The Library receives twenty-two thousand items each day and adds ten thousand to the collections.)
7. b.
8. True. The Library purchased it in 1930.
9. True. The book is *Old King Cole* and it measures $1/25'' \times 1/25''$. The pages can only be turned with the use of a needle.
10. James H. Billington.

Quiz 77: Famous American Women

1. Amelia Earhart.
2. Clara Barton.
3. Clare Boothe Luce.
4. Eleanor Roosevelt.
5. Elizabeth Seton.

6. Harriet Tubman.
7. Hillary Rodham Clinton.
8. Jacqueline Kennedy Onassis.
9. Rosa Parks.
10. Susan B. Anthony.

Quiz 78: The Top Ten American Religions

1,i; 2,c; 3,e; 4,a; 5,d; 6,f; 7,h,; 8,g; 9,b; 10,j. (Below is a list of the top ten religions ranked in order of number of members.)

1. Roman Catholic: 61,207,914.
2. Baptist: 33,064,341.
3. Methodist: 13,463,552.
4. Pentecostal: 10,396,628.
5. Lutheran: 8,312,036.
6. Islam: 5,500,000.
7. Latter-day Saints: 5,171,623.
8. Eastern Orthodox Churches: 5,058,998.
9. Presbyterian: 4,145,932.
10. Jewish: 4,075,000.

Quiz 79: American Superstitions

1. b.
2. d.
3. b,c.
4. c.

5. a.
6. a.
7. d.
8. b.

9. d.
10. b,d.

Quiz 80: Famous African-Americans

1. Hank Aaron.
2. Maya Angelou.
3. Louis Armstrong.
4. George Washington Carver.
5. Halle Berry.

6. Alex Haley.
7. Martin Luther King, Jr.
8. Condoleeza Rice.
9. Sojourner Truth.
10. Will Smith.

11. Tiger Woods.

12. Langston Hughes.

13. Oprah Winfrey.

14. Booker T. Washington.

15. Scott Joplin.

Quiz 81: American Disasters

1. False. "Although the story of Mrs. O'Leary's cow kicking over a coal oil-filled lantern has become part of American mythology, it has never been confirmed that the fire started in this manner. Several stories circulated after the fire about how it had begun and that was only one of them. Smoking hobos discarding their cigarettes carelessly were blamed, as was a visitor to the O'Leary home going to the barn for fresh milk and accidentally dropping a candle."[21]

2. Record-breaking amounts of snow, exceptionally high winds, and severely frigid temperatures.

3. The too-weak Johnstown Dam burst.

4. b.

5. a.

6. b.

7. True.

8. True.

9. Timothy McVeigh, who was executed for his crimes by lethal injection in 2001.

10. The two World Trade Center towers in New York City were taken down by planes hijacked by Islamic terrorists.

Quiz 82: Weird America

1. a.

2. Kenneth Arnold.

3. c.

4. True. He saw the UFO in October 1969 in Leary, Georgia. Of his sighting, he later said, "I am convinced that UFOs exist because I've seen one. . . . It was a very peculiar aberration, but about twenty people saw it. . . . It was the darndest thing I've ever seen. It was big; it was very bright; it changed colors; and it was about the size of the moon. We watched it for ten minutes, but none of us could figure out what it was . . ."[22]

5. True. A statement from NASA—Number FS-1997-01-017-HQ titled "The US Government and Unidentified Flying Objects" states "No branch of the United States Government is currently involved with or responsible for

investigations into the possibility of alien life on other planets or for investigating Unidentified Flying Objects (UFO's)." Whether or not you believe this is up to you.

6. c.

7. d. Although "Sasquatch" is mostly used in Canada, and "Yeti" in Asia.

8. Charles Fort.

9. g.

10. True.

Quiz 83: Native American Contributions to American Culture

1. Potatoes and sweet potatoes.
2. Tomatoes.
3. Quinine.
4. The tent.
5. The hammock.
6. The toboggan.
7. Ipecac.
8. Vanilla.
9. The moccasin.
10. The poncho.

Quiz 84: The Ultimate Red, White & Blue IQ Test

1. d.
2. c.
3. a.
4. b.
5. d.
6. d.
7. c.
8. c.
9. d.
10. b.
11. c.
12. b.
13. d.
14. b, g, i.
15. b.
16. c.
17. c.
18. a.

19. True.

20. False. It was founded that year, but by Alexander Hamilton.

21. False. The Court ruled that a Louisiana statute requiring that schools also teach creationism was a *violation* of the First Amendment.

22. All of the statements are true.

23. True.

24. False. The communications giant introduced rotary dialing twenty-five years prior to 1930, in 1905.

25. True. The Supreme Court issued this ruling in 1964 in the case *New York Times Company v. Sullivan.*

26. False. Even though Indians were not subject to the draft, many volunteered to serve and were accepted into the Armed Forces.

27. True.

28. False. That derogatory sobriquet was bestowed upon President Richard Nixon.

29. True. He was forty-three. (Teddy Roosevelt, however, was the youngest President ever to serve. He took office at the age of forty-three after the assassination of President McKinley.)

30. True.

31. False. The Department of Defense is part of the Executive Branch.

32. True. Did it work? Five Presidents elected in a year ending in a zero (Harrison; Lincoln, Garfield, Harding, Kennedy) died in office. President Reagan was shot in 1980, but survived, and experts on the paranormal believe that this successfully broke Tecumseh's curse.

33. 1. George Washington; 2. John Adams; 3. Thomas Jefferson; 4. James Madison; 5. James Monroe; 6. John Quincy Adams; 7. Andrew Jackson; 8. Martin Van Buren; 9. William Henry Harrison; 10. John Tyler; 11. James K. Polk; 12. Zachary Taylor; 13. Millard Fillmore; 14. Franklin Pierce; 15. James Buchanan; 16. Abraham Lincoln; 17. Andrew Johnson; 18. Ulysses S. Grant; 19. Rutherford B. Hayes; 20. James A. Garfield; 21. Chester A. Arthur; 22. Grover Cleveland; 23. Benjamin Harrison; 24. Grover Cleveland; 25. William McKinley; 26. Theodore Roosevelt; 27. William Howard Taft; 28. Woodrow Wilson; 29. Warren G. Harding; 30. Calvin Coolidge; 31. Herbert C. Hoover; 32. Franklin D. Roosevelt; 33. Harry S Truman; 34. Dwight D. Eisenhower; 35. John F. Kennedy; 36. Lyndon B. Johnson; 37. Richard M. Nixon; 38. Gerald R. Ford; 39. Jimmy Carter, Jr; 40. Ronald W. Reagan; 41. George H. W. Bush; 42. Bill Clinton; 43. George W. Bush.

34. 1. Delaware (12/7/1787); 2. Pennsylvania (12/12/1787); 3. New Jersey (12/18/1787); 4. Georgia (1/2/1788); 5. Connecticut (1/9/1788); 6. Massachusetts (2/6/1788); 7. Maryland (4/28/1788); 8. South Carolina (5/23/1788); 9. New Hampshire (6/21/1788); 10. Virginia (6/25/1788); 11. New York (7/26/1788); 12. North Carolina (11/21/1789); 13. Rhode Island (5/29/1790).

35. 1. Vice President; 2. Speaker of the House; 3. President Pro Tempore of the Senate; 4. Secretary of State; 5. Secretary of the Treasury; 6. Secretary of Defense; 7. Attorney General; 8. Secretary of the Interior; 9. Secretary of Agriculture; 10. Secretary of Commerce; 11. Secretary of Labor; 12. Secretary of Health and Human Services; 13. Secretary of Housing and Urban Development; 14. Secretary of Transportation; 15. Secretary of Energy; 16. Secretary of Education.

36. The book is *Turning Point* (Times Books, 1992) by Jimmy Carter.

37. Hancock.

38. Arms; Talks.

39. True.

40. False. He was released in September 1974 when a federal court overturned his 1971 conviction for the My Lai massacre.

41. Black Panthers.

42. Valley Forge, Pennsylvania.

43. The Gulf of Tonkin Resolution.

44. We purchased it from Russia and paid $7.2 million.

45. California (1), Texas (2), New York (3), Florida (4), Pennsylvania (5).

46. Wyoming (50), Vermont (49), Alaska (48), North Dakota (47), Delaware (46).

47. All of these men are astronauts who walked on the Moon.

48. Guam. It is the first U.S possession on which the sun rises.

49. They were all Vice Presidents of the United States.

50. Croatia, in 1776.

51. False. The flag at the White House is only flown when the President is in residence and then only from sunrise to sunset.

52. In 1954, by an Act of Congress.

53. a,c.

54. Vermont and Kentucky.

55. New Mexico and Arizona.

56. b.

57. Charles Thomson.

58. South Carolina, on December 20, 1860.

59. Peyton Randolph of Virginia, in 1774.

60. Woodrow Wilson.

61. Six: Gerald Ford, Jimmy Carter, Ronald Reagan, George Bush, Bill Clinton, and George W. Bush.

62. Virginia: George Washington (Westmoreland County); Thomas Jefferson (Albemarle County); James Madison (Port Conway); James Monroe (Westmoreland County); William H. Harrison (Berkeley); John Tyler (Greenway); Zachary Taylor (Orange County); Woodrow Wilson (Staunton).

63. The 1949 North Atlantic Treaty, which created NATO.

64. Patrick Henry, on March 20, 1775, at an assembly meeting at Richmond, Virginia.

65. Andrew Carnegie (November 25, 1835—August 11, 1919).

66. Martin Luther King, Jr.

67. True.

68. b.

69. William Henry Seward (May 16, 1801—October 10, 1872).

70. Samuel Houston (March 2, 1793—July 26, 1863).

71. False. He was born in Scotland.

72. Louis Armstrong.

73. Jane Addams (September 6, 1860—May 21, 1935).

74. Benjamin Franklin.

75. Edgar Allan Poe.

76. Amelia Earhart (July 24, 1897—July 2, 1937[?])

77. True. The seven Secretary-Generals of the U.N. to date are: Trygve Lie (Norway, 1946–1952); Dag Hammarskjold (Sweden, 1953–1961); U Thant (Myanmar [formerly Burma], 1961–1971); Kurt Waldheim (Austria, 1972–1981); Javier Pérez de Cueller (Peru, 1982–1991); Boutros Boutros-Ghali (Egypt, 1992–1996); Kofi Annan (Ghana, 1997–).

78. True.

79. The War Production Board.

80. *Stars and Stripes.*

Quiz 85: American Lasts

1. It was the last all-black regiment and its disbandment officially ended segregation in the United States military.

2. The Brooklyn Dodgers and the Pittsburgh Pirates. (The Dodgers won, 2-0.)

3. True. A black man was hung for the murder of a white woman. After the trap was sprung, the crowd swarmed Rainey Bethea's body for souvenirs. This put an end to public executions.

4. d.

5. a.

6. c. (Electricity was used in the White House for the first time during Benjamin Harrison's administration; Grover Cleveland lived without electricity for his first term, but had it for his second term, which commenced after Benjamin Harrison.)

7. b.

8. Candlestick Park, San Francisco, California, August 29, 1966.

9. d.

10. "all."

Notes

☆ ☆ ☆ ☆ ☆

1. Washington was not President at the time of the Revolutionary War, but he was the key figure in the war, and he went on to become the United States' first President.
2. *The Oxford Companion to American Military History*, John Whiteclay Chambers II, editor. (New York: Oxford University Press, 1999.)
3. All battles and dates drawn from *American Battlefields: A Complete Guide to the Historic Conflicts in Words, Maps, and Photos*, by Hubbard Cobb (Macmillan, 1995).
4. Ibid.
5. *The Oxford Companion to American Military History*, p. 410.
6. Ibid.
7. Ibid., p. 849.
8. Ibid., p. 849.
9. Ibid., p. 369.
10. Ibid., p. 371.
11. Speech by General William C. Westmoreland before the Third Annual Reunion of the Vietnam Helicopter Pilots Association (VHPA) at the Washington, D.C. Hilton Hotel on July 5, 1986 (reproduced in a *Vietnam Helicopter Pilots Association Historical Reference Directory* Volume 2A).
12. Speech by Lt. Gen. Barry R. McCaffrey (reproduced in the *Pentagram*, June 4, 1993), assistant to the Chairman of the Joint Chiefs of Staff, to Vietnam veterans and visitors gathered at "The Wall," Memorial Day 1993.
13. 1996 *Information Please Almanac*; Stephen J. Spignesi, *The U.S.A. Book of Lists*.
14. Gary Roush, former Vietnam helicopter pilot, www.vhfcn.org/stats.htm.; Stephen J. Spignesi, *The U.S.A. Book of Lists*.
15. Speech by General William C. Westmoreland before the Third Annual Reunion of the Vietnam Helicopter Pilots Association (VHPA) at the Washington, D.C. Hilton Hotel on July 5, 1986 (reproduced in a *Vietnam Helicopter Pilots Association Historical Reference Directory* Volume 2A).
16. The United States Supreme Court annulled Bell's patent in 1887 on the grounds of fraud and misrepresentation.
17. The original quotation should have been, "One small step for a man . . ." but Neil Armstrong omitted the "a" in his statement.
18. Library of Congress *Gettysburg Address* online exhibition.
19. *The Oxford Companion to American Military History*, p. 452.
20. John White, *The Pledge of Allegiance and The Star-Spangled Banner*.
21. Stephen Spignesi, *The 100 Greatest Disasters of All Time*.
22. *The National Enquirer*, June 8, 1976.

About the Author

☆ ☆ ☆ ☆ ☆

Stephen J. Spignesi is the author of numerous books on entertainment, popular culture, and historical biography, including *The Beatles Book of Lists*, *The Lost Work of Stephen King*, *The Complete Titanic*, *The Robin Williams Scrapbook*, *J.F.K. Jr.*, *The ER Companion*, *The Italian 100*, *The UFO Book of Lists*, *The Hollywood Book of Lists*, and *The 100 Greatest Disasters of All Time*. He lives in New Haven, Connecticut.